Pier Head Jump

Tommy Miller

Pharaoh Press

Pier Head Jump
ISBN 0 9525543 4 8

First Published in 1996 by Pharaoh Press, Roby, L36

Copyright © Tommy Miller 1996

The right of Tommy Miller to be identified as the author of
this work has been asserted in accordance with sections
77 and 78 of the Copyright, Designs and Patents Act
1988.

Typeset by
🄽🄴🄼🄾
Liverpool L3 4BD

Printed by
Cromwell Press,
Wiltshire

Acknowledgements

*My thanks to John O'Toole
for his constructive assistance
and co-operation with the
original manuscript*

*Thanks also to Billy and Wally
from Radio City in Liverpool
for their valuable support*

Chapter 1
Pier Head Jump

When I first left school I had no real ambition and no clear idea of what I wanted to do with my life. From St Philomena's School in Sparrow Hall, I'd gone into a few jobs that didn't add up to very much, probably because I wasn't that interested in them. My mother, Margaret, had heard there was a job for a willing lad in the Co-Op in Warbreck Moor, just down the road from Aintree Racecourse, and so I was packed off to see the manager, Mr Tyrer.

He was sufficiently impressed to give a start, and so I became the delivery-boy for the Co-Op on the princely sum of one pound five shillings a week. I got on well with the staff and the customers and I enjoyed the freedom of the job. I'd been there six weeks and loved it.

It was at that time that I came home one night to find my older brother, John, packing his sea-bag. He was married with three kids and was fifteen years older than me. He lived off Scotland Road, but had gone out "on the ale" with his old mates the previous night and never made it home. His bag was like a large canvas sack drawn together at the top by a cord running through steel-rimmed holes. I'd never been remotely interested in going to sea and watched him without interest.

"If you can get yourself down to the docks tomorrow," he told me, "I might have a few hundred cigs for me dad."

I said I would if I could.

The next day was Saturday, 2nd March 1947, and it was a typical English winter morning – cold, damp and pouring with rain. I'd already quietly decided I was going nowhere near the docks that day, I'd make sure I was too busy. I put on my overcoat, a huge greatcoat given to me by an A.R.P. Warden, still bearing its badges, when I heard my dad's voice booming from the kitchen.

"Don't come back here tonight without those cigarettes!"

My old man, Tony, was a ruthless man and you obeyed his every word. So that was that and no excuses.

That night was also to be my first date with May, who worked on the bread counter at the Co-Op. We were going to the Aintree Palace in Walton Vale (now the 'Shoemarket') to see Randolf Scott and Ella Raines in 'The Nelson Touch'. I really didn't want to cycle down to the Docks and back.

I arrived at the Co-Op at half-eight as usual, and after chatting to May for a couple of minutes, I started to load my bike. It was a huge 'sit up and beg' contraption that I could barely climb onto. The groceries were packed into a large wicker basket fixed to the front and I had about a dozen deliveries to make. I thought if I got a move on I could finish my round by half-four, get down to the docks and be back in plenty of time to see May. As I made my way out of the shop, I told her I'd see her later and pushed the bike in the direction of Park Lane. I could hardly be expected to know that twenty years would pass before I would see May again!

✱ ✱ ✱ ✱

It was just after four and I'd done well. I'd made all the deliveries except for one who was out, and I'd collected £3.10s.6d., which was another part of my job. I decided to leave the remaining order in the basket until the next day and set off for the Docks about five miles away. I was wet but resigned to what I had to do.

When I finally arrived at the Main Gate of the Alexandra Dock my way was barred by an enormous policeman, who wore a thick, dark moustache. Emerging from the warmth of the Gatehouse, he was none too pleased at being brought out into a wet and miserable afternoon by a young lad like me.

"Yes, young man, what can I do for you?"

I was hardly about to say I'd come to see my brother who had a few hundred ciggies for me dad! Instead, thinking as quickly as I could, I said, "I've got an order on my bike for a ship, sir!"

"Oh, aye." he answered abruptly and disbelievingly, "what's the name of this ship, then?"

"The *Empire McDermott*, sir."

He lifted up the flap of the basket and examined the butter, tea, sugar and side of bacon left over from my deliveries. "OK, lad," he nodded. "she's laying on the West Side."

I didn't have the faintest idea where the West Side was, but I moved off pretty sharpish! I asked a docker where it was, but he didn't seem to think I was worth an answer. I moved along the side of the quay with no idea which way to go. It was now well past five and if I didn't find this ship fairly soon I'd have to get going if I was to be back in time to meet May. At the time that seemed to be more important than the earful I'd get off my old man if I went home empty-handed.

It was now too dark and misty to ride the bike, so I struggled along on foot pushing it until I came across another docker. He was more helpful. "Go over the bridge there, son, she's laying on the West Wall. You'd better get a move n, she's all singled up and ready to sail."

I was later to learn that 'singled-up' meant all the ship's ropes had been taken in bar one fore and aft.

Over the bridge, laying along the side of the quay, was an old grey, rusty-looking aircraft carrier. This can't be it, I thought, this is a Royal Navy ship. John hadn't told me what kind of ship it was, but I couldn't believe it was this one. Just then, I came up to another docker who was making the most ridiculous attempts to get on his bike. He was obviously three sheets to the wind and had probably been working on a ship loading whisky. I lay my own bike on the floor and with a lot of huffing and puffing managed to help him get on. With blurred speech and flailing arms he told me that this was, indeed, the *Empire McDermott* and off he went. A few seconds later I heard an enormous clatter and good enough, he'd fallen off his bike again! He was going to be a long time getting home.

I stopped at the foot of the gangway and leaned my bike against a handy lamp-post. There was a lot of activity on board and she was clearly about to sail. There were seamen at the top of the gangway, standing by to let it go, and I shouted up if I could come aboard to get some cigarettes off my brother.

"What's his name?" he shouted back.

"John Miller." Luckily, my brother was within shouting distance, as the Chief Officer would not have let him leave his station. John's head appeared and he shouted down he wouldn't be a minute.

The seaman on the gangway called me on board just as the Dockmaster came along. The Captain, a big, thick-set man, shouted out, "Hold on to your ropes!" and looked down towards the Dockmaster. "What's happening?"

"There's a problem with one of the lock-gates", came the reply, "it should be right in about twenty minutes."

John came over with the cigarettes, a carton of 200 Canadian 'Sweet Caparelles'. I was about to leave when a short, stocky seaman with bright red hair – who turned out to be the ship's bosun – came along to tell the men what the hold-up was all about. He called my brother to one side and I waited to give a final "Cheerio". After a couple of minutes John came back and told me the Deck-Boy hadn't turned up and the Bosun had asked if I wanted his job!

"You've got about five minutes to make your mind up."

Suddenly, my mind was in a turmoil. For one thing, my bike was still on the quayside and I had £3.10s.6d. in my pocket belonging to the Co-Op. On top of this, May would be waiting outside the picture-house. At that moment, the Dockmaster returned and called up to the Captain that the Lock-Gate had been repaired. Before I could move the order came crackling over the tannoy ... "Let the gangway go!" I turned in a panic, but the gangway had already gone. Once the weight was taken off the ropes it dropped to the floor in seconds. It seemed everybody was shouting.

"Let go fore and aft!" "Hold on to your spring rope!"

And then the final order ...

"Let go all!"

The Chief Mate called from the bow, "All gone fore'd!"

The Captain called, "Let go of your tug aft!" And the next thing I knew we were clear of the Lock and steaming up the River Mersey bound for Montreal!

✳✳✳✳

In those days, a Pier Head Jump was a common thing and the term applied to wherever on the line of Liverpool's docks it happened. 'Landlubbers' thought it applied to those who jumped on the ship as it set sail. In practice, it only happened when a seaman failed to join the ship and someone happened to be there to take his place. This time, that someone was me!

Most 'jumpers' had no experience and no skills applicable to seafaring. All I could do was ride a bike! Anyway, I had to sign the Ship's Articles and I became a member of the crew. Normally a first tripper would sail as a Deck Boy or a Ship's Peggy, who had the job of fetching the seamen's food from the Galley to the Mess Room and cleaning the Mess, the toilets and so on. Instead, I was thrown in at the deep end and put on 12-4 Watch, and not being able to steer did the four-hour long look-out!

Luckily, I was on the same Watch as John and his best mate, 'Nutty' Curran. 'Nutty' was about twenty stone and always slept on a bottom bunk as nobody fancied their chances of sleeping underneath him. John had known him for years. They'd served in the Royal Navy together during the war and joined the Merchant Navy at the same time.

If ever there was any trouble I knew whose side I was on! Our John was six foot two and slim but solid. He wasn't a bad-looking bloke and would have looked a lot better only for the scars he'd picked up around the world! This was to be his last trip as he'd been offered a good shore job as a ship's rigger when he got back. 'Nutty' was an appropriate nickname for John's mate because he was a complete nutter. He had his huge head shaved like Yul Bryner with a five pointed star tattooed on each ear. His teeth were so decayed he had more use for a brillo-pad than a toothbrush. For all that, he had a heart of gold.

By half-past-eleven we were approaching Point Lynas where

we dropped off the Pilot. The ship's telegraph rang 'All Stop' and the Third Mate of the Watch called to the seaman on the fore'd deck. "OK, lower your rope ladder!" The Pilot Cutter was laying off about half a mile away and their gig-boat was lowered and came across to pick up the Pilot. Although the sea was getting up and the ship beginning to roll, the Pilot − a big enough man − skipped over the ship's rail and dropped down the rope ladder like a two-year-old. "Have a good trip, sir!"

Even the apprentice pilots had to be admired for the way they handled the small gig-boats in rough weather. I was brought back to reality with another ringing of the ship's telegraph and one long blast of the ship's whistle − a salute to the Pilot.

At midnight, eight bells, I had to go on watch. Our John took the wheel and I went on the Monkey-Island on top of the wheelhouse to relieve the look-out man. 'Nutty' was on stand-by in case the Mate of the Watch needed him. My instruction in look-out duty was hardy detailed. The seaman I was replacing pointed to a small bell.

"When you see a ship to Starboard," he said, "you ring one bell. You see a ship to port your ring two bells. You see a ship dead ahead you ring three bells."

Starboard? Port?

"Always remember which is which. Starboard is to your right and Port to your left."

I nodded.

"By the way, they call me Bubbles. What's your name?"

"Tommy."

"OK, Tommy, I'm going below for a good kip. I've been on the beer all day and I'll sleep like a log. Good luck!"

And he was gone. Bubbles, I thought, what a nickname! He was a colossal bloke with a face that looked as it had had come across Rocky Marciano in a bad mood! He didn't look like a 'Bubbles' to me. Apparently, when he was born he was a big bouncing baby and the name stuck. At least that's what I was told.

By now, we were clearing the shoreline and the shore lights were disappearing from view. My God, I thought to myself, what am I doing here? I was still wearing my A.R.P. Warden's overcoat, my Co-Op apron and my money-bag. I was truly 'parish dressed and schooner rigged'!

The sea was getting rough, the wind blowing stronger and the ship was starting to roll heavily. 'Nutty' came up to the Monkey-Island with a mug of cocoa.

"Get this down yer, lad!" he said with a friendly smile, "it'll do yer the world of good. We're heading into a force ten gale."

I didn't have a clue what a force ten gale was, but I wasn't much older when I found out! The ship rolled more violently and did everything but turn over. I was as sick as a dog.

The *Empire McDermott*, being an aircraft carrier, was a light ship and couldn't really stand up to this. She was one of several acquired by the Merchant Service after the war to run grain from Halifax and Montreal to Liverpool. They had one large hold, which had once been a hangar and now carried 10,000 tons of grain. By three-o'clock I felt I'd spent half my life on look-out and as John had been relieved on the wheel he came up to give me a break and have a smoke. He took one look at me. "How do you feel?"

"Bloody rough! Is there a chance you can ask the Captain to stop the ship and let me off?"

He smiled. "It's a bit late for that now. You'll be alright in a few days when the weather gets a bit better." He gave me a slap on the arm. "Get yourself below. I'll finish your watch for you."

I stumbled off and found my way below. There were four bunks to a cabin and I just fell on the nearest, and wearing the A.R.P. coat, apron, money-bag and all, passed out.

The next thing I remember was being shaken at twenty-past-eleven the next day. It was Jacko from Nottingham. "Come on, Dusty! It's seven bells! Time to get yerself ready and go on watch!"

I struggled to my feet and made my way out towards the Mess Room to get some dinner. Jacko watched me with a huge grin on his face. I was still wearing my bicycle clips!

Chapter 2
Unsung Heroes

I felt dreadful. Jacko called after me laughing. "Get some dinner down yer, Dusty! It's pork chops in loads of sloppy fat!" I headed for the toilet but never made it. I threw open the nearest port hole and stuck my head through. I was violently sick, and as luck would have it, I was up-wind and got the lot back! Jacko had been going to sea for more than ten years and didn't get seasick, but he took one look and me and went right off the idea of pork-chops. It was some consolation.

After a quick wash, my first since leaving Liverpool, I made my way to the Mess Room, but I could barely manage a cup of tea. The boys were ignoring the weather and getting stuck into their dinner. There was a force ten blowing and I spilt more tea than I drank.

At mid-day, eight bells, I went up on Watch, but there wasn't much seamanship to be done. Nutty relieved the man at the ship's wheel and me and our kid were sent below to wash the paintwork in the alleyways. Towards the end of the shift, the Bosun, an Irishman, came along.

"Right, young Dusty, put your bucket away and take yourself off for a shower. When you're done, come down to the Slop Chest and we'll get you rigged out in some proper gear. You'll have to pay for it, but not to worry, it'll be taken out of your wages at the end of the trip. Go on, lad, away you go!"

This was something of an experience for me because I'd never had a shower before. Like most people in those days I was used to a tin bath in front of the fire. I spent about five minutes working out what knobs went which way. First it was scalding hot and then freezing cold. Finally I got it right and settled into the luxury of a hot, soapy shower for the first time. It was to be the first of too many to count.

✳ ✳ ✳ ✳

I made my way down to the Bound where the ABs and 'donkey greasers' were getting their tobacco issue. I didn't smoke at that time so I loaded up with all kinds of boiled sweets and chocolate. The man in charge of both the Bound and the Ship's Chest was 'Taffy' Jones, the first Welshman I'd ever met.

"Right, boyo. I believe you're the first tripper, so what I'll do, see, is issue you with two shirts and two pairs of dungarees. The shirts are seven and six and the dungarees twelve shillings. Do you have that, boyo?"

The only money I had was the £3.10s.6d belonging to the Co-Op and that was stashed away under my mattress. I shook my head.

"Not to worry, boyo, just sign here. There's lovely!"

The weather had become calmer and, fitted out in my new rig I was really beginning to feel like one of the boys. After a few days, I was allowed to steer the ship without supervision and at midnight on my fourth night, I took the first wheel of the watch. 'Mungo', from the south end of Liverpool, had been at the wheel when I came on. He'd been going to sea for about eight years and was a J.O.S. – a Junior Ordinary Seaman.

"OK, young Dusty, she's all yours. She's steering like a son of a bitch, I'm afraid, we've got the sea up our arse!"

This was a blunt way of saying the tide was behind the ship. He gave me the ship's course and told me how much wheel she was carrying and repeated the same to the Mate of the Watch. On the *Empire McDermott* the Mate was on the Top-Bridge and the Wheel-Man on the Lower-Bridge. All communication was done by voice-pipe. You were very much on your own, but if you steered four or five degrees off course the Mate would let you know soon enough.

After an hour I was joined by the Second Mate of the Watch, a real gentleman.

"How are you getting on, young man?" he said.

"Fine, sir." I replied with great respect. He was from the Bristol area and looked more like a bomber pilot than a seaman. He was about six foot six and nearly bald, but he had a handlebar moustache that almost touched his earlobes. He wore a leather jacket with a massive fur collar and looked completely out of place.

"Right!" he said. "Keep up the good work, I'll be keeping my eye on you."

I did my two hour trick with no problems and before I knew it, Nutty arrived as my relief. I gave him the course and repeated it to the Second Mate, 'Handlebar.'

"Thank you, Miller, you're getting better."

Nutty told me there was a pot of tea and a 'sarny' in the Mess Room. I made my way below and without the other two Watches around it was pleasantly quiet.

I was enjoying my break when the buzzer sounded, which meant I was wanted up on the Bridge. As I made my way back, fog was beginning to descend on the ship. Handlebar was waiting for me.

"The Captain will be on the bridge in a few minutes. Go down to the pantry, you will find a round tray, a tea-pot and some sugar. Make a pot of tea and bring it back to me."

I had only heard the Captain referred to as 'Skipper' or 'The Old Man' by the lads and on the few days I'd been on the ship I'd never spoken to him. When I got back, both the Captain and Handlebar were in the Chart Room, leaning on a table and making corrections on the chart. I set the tray down on the table and started to pour the tea.

"How many sugars, Skipper?" I asked, quite cheerfully.

The Captain turned and glared at me with a murderous look in his eyes. I froze. I didn't know what I had done.

"Young man!" he thundered, "it is your first trip and I am going to give you the benefit of the doubt. You will never again address me as 'Skipper'! You will find 'skippers' on fishing boats, tugs and private yachts. This, young man, is a ship and I am her Master Captain! I would, however, prefer that you address me as 'Sir'. Do I make myself perfectly clear?"

I could barely speak. "Yes, sir!" I croaked.

"Thank you, young man, I do not take sugar."

I finished pouring the tea and stole a glance at Handlebar, who was paralysed rigid for fear that he would burst out laughing.

"Just one for me, thank you," he stuttered. I told John about it later and the lads all thought it was hysterical. "At least you never called him 'Old Man'," he laughed, "he'd have chucked you over the side!"

I had to go along with all the leg-pulling. It was a lesson learnt and I could see the funny side. In a quiet moment, no doubt the Captain would, too.

The Captain was a much respected man by the crew. During the war he had been torpedoed several times when carrying a cargo of petroleum spirit. He looked a lot older than he was, but given his history it was hardly surprising. Most of the men on board had seen action of some sort or another. Only myself and a lad from Glasgow had no experience of running the Atlantic with U-Boats menacing every moment. He was known as 'The Flying Flea' after he had been asked what he'd been doing in port. "Oh, just hopping around the bars," he said.

'Bugsy' Boyle was torpedoed on his first trip across the Atlantic and spent the rest of the war as a P.O.W. in Germany. The Second Cook was an Italian, Marcello Riossi, an anti-fascist who had married a Liverpool girl. We called him 'Mike' and everybody loved him. He made fresh ice-cream on board and to this day it's still the best I've ever tasted! He also made the bread, but that was dreadful. 'Ship's Ballast' we called it.

"Oh, thatsa very funny!" he used to say, "maybe you canna do ita better, eh?"

"Mike," our John said, "I could make better bread with plasticine!"

We had a good laugh at Mike's expense, but he always gave as good as he got.

The Chief Cook was a happy-go-lucky sort of bloke who didn't really talk about the war. His main problem, or everybody else's really, was his feet! Those who had the misfortune to share his cabin reckoned you could soak his feet in Channel N°5 for a week and they'd still stink!

Of all the crew, the Chief Mate had had the worst experience. He was a quiet, pleasant man from Eastbourne, who had been badly burned. He'd had quite extensive plastic surgery, which had been very successful, except that his face was drawn into an almost permanent smile. It was difficult to know whether or not he was actually in good mood. Apparently, he had been on a ship carrying ammunition which had suffered a direct hit from a German bomber. From a crew of fifty-six seaman he was one of only four who survived.

The war had ended less than two years earlier and they all had their hair-raising stories of near-misses and narrow escapes. Many of their friends had lost their lives. It had been a grim time and for those unsung heroes of the Battle of the Atlantic it was never very far away from their thoughts.

Chapter 3
Land Ahoy!

I was in the Mess Room learning to play Cribbage when the Bosun put his head around the door.

"Boat Drill at four-thirty so make sure you've all got a life jacket on."

I was shown how to put one on and at spot on half-four, the drill for 'Abandoned Ship' started with a continuous ringing of the ship's alarm bells. This was followed by six short blasts on the ship's whistle then one long one. The ship's whistle would be better described to somebody who hasn't been away to sea as a 'fog horn'.

We were quickly on deck and mustered at our Boat Station – Nº4. Our names were ticked off the roll call by the Third Mate. All the port and starboard boats were efficiently swung out on the davits and lowered about four feet. They were swung back in again, fixed and the Boat Drill was over. The ship's whistle was then sounded for the Fire Drill; one blast for 'Fire Fore', two blasts for 'Fire Amidship', and three blasts for 'Fire Aft'.

The following day we were covered in a blanket of fog and had to double-up on the look-out, one man on the Monkey Island and one on the Bridge. The ship's whistle blew every few seconds. The ship's engines were given 'Dead Slow Ahead' and that's how we progressed for the next twenty-four hours.

When the fog finally lifted, the engines were put on 'Full Ahead' but the telegraph was kept on stand-by as you could never be sure the fog wouldn't come straight down again. The weather was cold and damp and my A.R.P. overcoat was worth its weight in gold. It hadn't gone unnoticed. Nutty turned to our John, "By the time we get back to Liverpool," he said laughing, "your Tommy's gonna need surgery to get that coat off his back!"

We were twelve days out of Liverpool and in two days time would be in Montreal. There had still been no word home. To begin with, I'd been under the impression that John was sending a ship's telegram. That hadn't happened and when I brought the subject up, he just shrugged his shoulders.

"Don't worry, they'll have a good idea where you are, you can send a letter when we get to Montreal."

And that was it. As I found out a couple of weeks later, there was a lot of anxiety at home.

★ ★ ★ ★

The weather was getting warmer and the Watch on deck were giving the paintwork a washing down to look smart when we got to Canada. In fact, the ship was an R.N. grey and didn't seem to look much different to me. On the fourteenth day I was on the Monkey Island look-out and in a world of my own. I was thinking about what might be going on back home and about May, who would have been less than pleased when I hadn't turned up. My day-dreaming came to an abrupt end with the clatter of Handlebar's boots on the Monkey Island steps.

"Right, young man. Very soon there should be a flashing light about two-points on the starboard bow. When you see it, let me know. Is that clear?"

"Yes, sir!"

"Thank you. Keep a sharp look-out."

By this time I was familiar with most of the points of the compass. From the starboard bow to the starboard wing of the Bridge was eight points. The port bow to the port wing on the Bridge was another eight.

Twenty minutes later there it was! On the starboard bow I saw a light on the horizon for the first time in two weeks. It was also the first light I'd had to report to the Officer of the Watch. I rang 'One Bell', but to make sure I took the flap off the voice-pipe and called "Flashing light, two points on the starboard bow."

Handlebar called back, "Thank you!" And a few minutes later he appeared on the Monkey Island. He removed the binnacle off the top of the compass and took a bearing off the light.

The following day I came up on deck and there before me was land – my first sight of a foreign country, Canada. In all my life I had never seen such beauty. As I gazed in wide-eyed astonishment, the rest of the crew took it for granted. We had entered the Strait of Belle Isle which separates the island of Newfoundland from the Canadian mainland. On the port side we passed the island towns of Cook's Harbour and Flowers Cove and on the starboard side West Saint Modeste and Blanc Sablon. We steered for Father Point to pick up the Pilot. The Strait opened up into the Gulf of Saint Lawrence, but we followed the Canadian coastline past Iles Monger, Ile D'Anticosti, Cap Whittle and Sept Iles. The old hands who had been here many times before and knew the charts were happy to give me these magical, alien names.

The engines were put on 'Dead Slow' and the pilot cutter skilfully manoeuvred alongside. The telegraph rang out and the engines put at 'All Stop'. The Jacob's Ladder was lowered over the side and made fast and the AB of the Watch lowered his heaving line. One of the crew tied, or bent, on the Pilot's gear. As at home, there was a Pilot and an apprentice. The Pilot was an Anglo-Canadian but the apprentice was a French-Canadian. Apparently, if the Pilot was one, the apprentice was the other and it was the official policy of the Canadian Government. The engines were put on 'Full Ahead' and we made our way up the St Lawrence River.

Seamen had nicknamed this stretch of water the 'River of a Thousand Churches'. You couldn't argue. There were too many to count and looking at the map you will find the small towns of Sainte-Marthe-de-Gaspe, Sainte-Anne-des-Monts, Sainte Felicite, Saint Leandre, Saint Eloi and a dozen more. We passed the larger towns of Baise-Comear, Hauterive and Betsiamiles on the starboard side and Matane Rimouski and Riviere-du-Loup to the port.

Along the river there were several islands, the largest of which was L'ile d'Orleans. As the river narrowed we came upon the beautiful city of Quebec, the former capital of Canada. All this was an education to me as I really hadn't had a proper one. I spent more time in an air-raid shelter than I did in a classroom and the only homework I did was collecting shrapnel from bombsites. We were now very close to the shoreline at Quebec and there, on the starboard side, was the most magnificent building I had ever seen – Le Chateau Frontenac, an exclusive hotel for the rich and famous.

I was now on Watch, but due to the strong current of the St Lawrence River and the difficulty in steering, I was too inexperienced to take the wheel. Instead, I helped fetch the mooring ropes from the rope locker in readiness for docking at Montreal. Spirits were high. Some of the lads had girlfriends in Montreal and this was the main topic of conversation. From Quebec to Montreal took the best part of five hours, passing the city of Trois-Rivieres, and at noon on Monday 18th March the ship was finally tied up and the gangway lowered. First aboard were the ship's agents, followed by the Customs and Immigration Officers.

I knew nothing of docking procedures and I thought after a few minutes we would get changed and go ashore. After an age we were finally cleared by the Customs Officers, but then the

Immigration Officers took their turn and asked each of us a few questions.

"Have you ever been arrested in Canada?"

"No sir, I've never been to Canada before."

"Have you ever been brought back to your shop under escort?"

"No sir, I've never been ..."

"Have you ever been deported from Canada?"

"No sir."

Eventually they were done and one of the lads came into the Mess Room and called "Sub up!" The Officers and Engineers were each given $20, the ABs $10 and the S.O.S., J.O.S. and myself $5. I went ashore with Jacko, who was nearest my age, and had been here a few times before.

First of all we went with John and Nutty to 'Joe Beef's Bar'. Some of the lads had gone to the 'Liverpool Bar' or the 'Vokland Club' on the St Lawrence Main. All seamen of the Canadian Pacific, Manchester and Cunard Lines will remember these places.

I didn't have a taste for beer in those days, but I was able to change the Co-Op money for Canadian dollars in Joe Beef's Bar. I would be able to pay that back out of my wages at the end of the trip, but for now it meant that, as I walked along the quay with Mungo, that I had nearly $20 in my pocket – the best part of £5. In those days I was a millionaire!

Chapter 4
Montreal

As we walked along the quay we passed the *Empress of Scotland* and I thought she was surely the biggest ship in the world. She had three huge yellow funnels with red and white chequered panels in the centre of each. They were an overwhelming sight, but little did I know that one day I would be hanging from a Bosun's chair painting those very same funnels.

Laying in the harbour was a forest of ships loading and off-loading their cargo. They included the *Beaverburn* of the Canadian Pacific, the *Assyria* of the Cunard Line, and the *Manchester Spinner* of the Manchester Line. The *Empire McDermott* incidentally, belonged to Hines Steamship Company.

Another company of the day was The Head Boats – a Belfast firm, managed by the Ulster Steamship Company. Their black funnels incorporated a white shield with the red hand of Ulster dripping blood from the wrist. One of the old timers, assisted by a half-bottle of rum, had told me a dubious story of its origin.

"Well, lad, an old man owned the company and he had two

sons who he loved the same. He was getting old and wanted to retire. He wanted to leave the company to one of his two sons because he believed only one man could be boss. Rather than leave it to the oldest lad, he decided it should go to the fittest and most determined. He was at his wit's end trying to sort it out and then he thought of a plan.

"In the bay there were two rowing boats and he told them they would race to an island about a mile away. 'The first one' he said 'to set hand or foot on the island is the winner and will own my company'.

"The following morning the young men took the boats and, with a witness and starter, the race began. They were neck and neck, first the older lad was a half length up and then his brother drew level and inched ahead. It was nip and tuck all the way, but as they neared the island, the younger brother proved the fitter and stronger and started to build a lead.

"The older brother had dreamed all his life of owning the family firm and gave out a cry of anguish as he saw defeat was inevitable. Just then he saw an axe under his seat. He grabbed the axe, dropped to his knees and with his brother only feet from the beach, brought the axe down with a crash onto his left wrist. Screaming in agony he picked up the severed hand and threw it onto the shore just seconds before his brother got there.

"The younger brother got out of his boat, looked at the hand, looked at his brother and remembered his father's words ... 'the first one to set hand or foot on the island is the winner.' His brother had won and owned the company."

"Blimey!" I said. "I thought he was going to kill his brother."

"He couldn't lad, could he? There were witnesses, he'd have been hanged and won nothing."

"What did his dad say?"

"Who knows, lad, but his eldest son wanted everybody to know what he'd given to own the company."

I never did find out what truth there was in that story, probably none, but as a sixteen year old still wet behind the ears, I was happy to believe it.

★ ★ ★ ★

The next thing I had to do was send a postcard home. Jacko knew his way around and took me to The Flying Angel, the Seaman's Mission in Montreal. I bought a card and a stamp and wrote a few lines including when I expected to get back to Liverpool. I felt better as soon as I'd posted it. At The Angel they were holding a dance for the seamen in port, but there seemed to be more crewmen from the *Empress of Scotland* than from all the other ships put together. There were a mixture of Anglo- and French-Canadian girls there, all having a good time.

We stayed for a few minutes and then headed 'down town'. The first person we saw who we knew was Jock, the Flying Flea. He'd obviously been doing his best to live up to his nickname as he staggered down the St Lawrence Main. By the state of him he must have been to every bar within a five mile radius. He looked at the pair of us and screwed his eyes as if he was sure he'd seen us somewhere before. He tried to walk towards us but his legs wouldn't go with him and at that moment a Police patrol car pulled up alongside him. As we walked on, we could hear Jock cursing and blowing as he was bundled into the back of the car and driven off.

We came into St Catherine's Street which was full of shops and when I looked in their windows I'd never seen anything like it. The street was full of flashing neon lights and wherever you looked there were cinemas and nightclubs. We went into a Milk Bar and ordered two milk-shakes and two hamburgers. I'd never tasted milk-shake before and nobody made hamburgers as good as the Americans and Canadians. By the time we left, we'd had about six milk-shakes and three hamburgers each!

Fit to burst we rolled into the street and with my new wealth decided to do some shopping. I bought myself a zip-up jacket, a pair of slacks, a couple of shirts and a pair of shoes. I bought some presents to take home and then we made our way back to the ship.

By the main entrance to the docks was a Fish and Chip shop with a world-wide reputation. Owned by 'Ma the Greek', it had greasy walls, peeling wallpaper and spiders webs hanging from the ceiling, but she made the best fish and chips you ever tasted. There were a dozen respectable restaurants in the area, but seamen walked past them to go to Ma the Greeks. On the *Empress of Scotland* I heard of a cabin steward who had been coming to Montreal for six years, but the only part of the city he had seen was Ma the Greeks. He'd finish work, walk across the road to Ma's and then take his fish and chips back to the ship to eat. As he was tucking in one of the lads quipped, "Fancy going all the way to bloody Montreal for a bag of fish and chips!"

★ ★ ★ ★

On board the following morning, the hangars were opened, grain shutes lowered and grain began to flow into the hold. We were turned to by the Bosun to do various jobs, but mostly we were washing the grain dust off the decks and bulk-heads. Four of the crew were adrift, but by mid-day three had turned up with big grins on their faces. Even at my age I didn't need telling twice what they'd been up to. The only member of the crew still missing, was of course, the Flying Flea and later in the day, the Bosun was told he was locked up and would be until the ship was ready to leave. It took six days to load the cargo and finally the hangars were closed and we were ready to go to sea. All hands were busy washing down. The grain was more like mud and took an age to clear.

Just before we were about to leave a police car pulled up at the foot of the gangway and the Flea was placed on board and firmly told if he ever set foot on Canadian soil again he'd be locked up straight away. According to the police, he'd been a right handful. He was told by the Bosun he was wanted on the Bridge at ten-thirty. The Captain deducted from him five days pay for being absent from work and fined him ten shillings for each day he'd been absent without leave. He was an S.O.S. and this represented a serious chunk of his wages, which was about £18.10s a month. After being logged, he came pounding down the decks calling the Captain fit to burn and giving the Bosun the same for reporting him. After going five days AWOL I'm sure the Bosun had no choice.

That wasn't the end of Jock's problems. He'd slept with a girl in Montreal, though nobody could work out how he'd found the time, and was showing the first signs of having to pay a visit to the Seaman's Dispensary when he got back to Liverpool. He was in good company. Two of the three lads who came back late smiling like Cheshire cats had both been going on about the beautiful girls they had been with. One was even saying he was going to quit the ship in Liverpool and go straight back to Montreal to get married. Their tune changed a few days later when the tell-tale signs appeared. You couldn't repeat what they were calling the girls now! "Wedding's off then, fellas?" Nutty shouted over.

Some of the lads were talking about their experiences when going to the Dispensary for a check-up. The entrance was directly opposite a sack warehouse, known as the 'baggy' in Canning Place. Inside were employed about two hundred women and it was impossible to get into the Dispensary without dozens of girls jeering at you.

"What 'ave you been up to, then?"

"Serves yer right, yer dirty ticket!"

"That'll teach yer!"

Most of the seamen went for their precautionary check-up if they thought they might need one before returning to wives and girlfriends. As far as the girls were concerned everybody was a positive case. There were even stories of lads going with their arm in a sling or with a bandage on their head, but it didn't do any good.

"I know you, Joey Riley, yer don't kid me in yer bandages!"

★ ★ ★ ★

With a belly full of grain we were low in the water and homeward bound. There should be no repeat performance of the outward trip. My God, I hoped not! Two days out of Montreal the weather was beautiful and the sea calm. I was going home at last and I had a story or two to tell when I got there. No doubt, I thought, I'd get an earful off me mam for disappearing the way I did, but I chuckled when I thought of me dad. I could just imagine walking in the door five weeks after I'd pushed my bike out into the rain.

"There you are, you little sod!" he'd say. "Yer took yer time with them bleedin' ciggies, didn't yer!"

Chapter 5
The Wanderer
Returns

As we entered Liverpool Bay there was a sense of anticipation amongst the lads. No matter where in the world they had been there was nothing like coming back into Liverpool. For those of us who lived in Liverpool the feelings were all the more intense.

It was a beautiful evening. The sky was a deep blue, the sea was calm and Spring was just around the corner. On the horizon, barely visible at first, the city gradually presented itself. Just a few weeks earlier I had seen what I believed to be the most beautiful building in the world – Le Chateau Frontenac. I was wrong. Coming down the Mersey, past Waterloo and Seacombe, alongside the Port of Liverpool Building and the Cunard Building, stood the elegant grace of the famous Liver Building. The two famous birds look down on the port as if keeping a protective vigil over its activities.

At that moment, I could have wept with joy. I had seen that building so many times before. Coming home from New

Brighton on the ferry after countless day-trips, I had looked at it as I did then. I never realised it was so beautiful. All Liverpool seafarers will recognise this feeling I describe. The Liver Building symbolised everything we felt about home.

After what seemed an eternity we entered Alexandra Dock through the Lock Gates and amid much noise and commotion we tied up. The gangway was lowered and aboard came the Customs Officer and the Shipping Master. As a 'home' ship, customs were very much a formality and we took it in turn to see the Shipping Master who paid the men off. I had over £3 docked form my wages for the dungarees and shirts I'd bought and the 'sub' I'd had in Montreal. I also deducted £3.10s.6d from myself to give back to the Co-Op. It didn't leave me with a great deal, but it was still a lot more than I was used to.

I came down the gangway with John and Nutty and looked across to the post where I'd left my bike.

"Me bike's gone!" I said.

John and Nutty both laughed.

"Yer can't trust anybody, can yer lad!" Our John said and Nutty pulled an expression of mock disgust.

"What's the world coming to, eh? Yer run a few errands, yer leave yer bike leaning against a lamp-post and yer come back five weeks later and some buggers had it away!"

"The Co-Op won't think it's funny," I moaned.

"I shouldn't worry, Tommy," our John said, putting an arm around my shoulder, "they'll have forgotten all about it by now."

John and Nutty were going for a few drinks before going home, but I was keen to get straight back. There were hackney cabs lining the quayside and carried away by my new-found wealth I decided to take one. I'd never been in a cab before in my life and in other circumstances the driver would have either thrown a lad my age straight out of the cab or asked me to pay up-front. But he knew I'd just been paid and I rode home like royalty returning from exile.

As I got close to home I was getting excited at the thought of seeing everyone again, but I wasn't sure what kind of reception I was going to get. As I got out of the cab our front door opened and my mother ran down the path like I was coming home from the Front. She hugged me like only mothers' can and I went inside to much shouting and leg-pulling. I was dressed in the new clothes I'd bought in Montreal and me dad took one look at me.

"Bloody 'ell! It's the Cunard Yank!" he gave me a smile and a friendly cuff over the head. "Last time I send you on a bloody message!"

We all laughed, except me mam who wasn't quite ready to laugh yet. My brothers Tony, Martin and Christie were there and also our Margaret, Theresa and Kathleen. I gave them all the presents I'd bought in Montreal, which of course included two hundred cigs for me dad. Me mam was starting to calm down.

"Oh, Tommy, we were all so worried 'til we got your card," she said.

"What happened, mam?"

"Well, when you never came home for your tea I wasn't too worried because I knew you were going out. When you never came home at all I was up all night worried sick. In the morning I went straight over to Aintree to the Co-Op, hoping to God you'd stayed out all night and gone straight to work. Anyway, I saw Mr Tyrer who hadn't see you and at first he wasn't very pleasant at all. He thought you'd run off with the delivery money. The young girl you were meeting ... I can't remember her name?"

"May," I said.

"Yes, May. She said you hadn't turned up at the Palace the night before, so then I just went straight to Rice Lane Police Station. They hadn't heard anything, but said they'd look into it. Anyway, a few hours later a bobby came round to the house and. Oh, God, Tommy, I feared the worst. He said they'd found your bike at the side of the Alexandra Dock. The bobby at the gatehouse remembered seeing you go into the docks but said you definitely hadn't come out.

"The weather was terrible that night, if you remember, and he said they were looking into the possibility that you'd fell in the dock. 'It does happen, Madam' he said. I was beside myself."

I could see tears welling up in me mam's eyes. "You didn't really think I'd fell in, did yer, mam?"

"I didn't know what to think, Tommy. Your dad had you right. "Pier Head Jump' he said. 'He's gone down there, they've been short-handed and he's gone with the ship. He's with our John.' he said. 'Oh Tony, I hope you're right!' I said and that's how it was until we got your card last week."

"Last week?" I couldn't believe it. "I sent that card three weeks ago."

"You sent it from Montreal, lad," me dad said, "that card came home the same speed you did."

"I'm sorry, mam."

"Well, as long as you're alright, son. Are you hungry?"

"Yes, mam. I'm starving."

"Well, thank God some things don't change!"

★ ★ ★ ★

The next morning I made my way by bus down to the Co-Op, about two miles from our house. I had to go and pay back the money I owed, but I was far more apprehensive about seeing May. Like a lot of sixteen year olds I was terrified of girls and my imagination ran riot at what she'd say to me. All the way there, I acted out in my mind every possible scenario and what I should say if she said this or she said that.

I finally arrived at the shop, lifted the latch and walked in. The familiar smell of fresh bread, meat and cleanliness hit me as if I'd never been away. Mr Tyrer, a plumb balding man in his forties, was at the top of a step-ladder, removing a tin from one of the high shelves. Dressed in his white Co-Op overall jacket, he looked over his shoulder and the top of his glasses.

"Ah! The wanderer returns!" he said. Holding a tin of peaches like a precious stone, he came down the steps and smiled at me. "Good morning, Master Miller."

"Good morning, Mr Tyrer." I answered a little sheepishly.

"And how was Canada?" News that I was home had travelled fast.

"Very good, sir."

"You left it where you found it?"

"Yes, sir."

"You have something for me?"

"Yes, Mr Tyrer."

"Very good."

I handed the money to him, correct to the penny and I was looking about for a sign of May. One of the women who worked there came over.

"Hello, Tommy."

"Hello, Ann."

"Are you looking for May?"

"Er, no, not really."

"She's left."

Left! I hadn't covered this. My first reaction was to wonder what I'd done. She must have been so angry she couldn't face me and left the following day. It obviously showed. "Oh, has she?" I stuttered.

"Don't worry, Tommy, it was nothing to do with you. Her dad got promoted at work and they've all moved down to Southampton."

Well, blow me! Who could have foreseen this at a time when most people hardly ever ventured from the area where they were born. A few week's ago we'd made a date. Two weeks later I was in Montreal and a week or so after that, May was living in Southampton. Clearly, we were never meant to be. God had gone to great lengths to make sure me and May never became sweethearts!

Chapter 6
New York! New York!

Before I left the shop, Mr Tyrer told me he was relieved when he found out I wasn't a thief.

"How did you know, sir? I asked him.

"Well, when I got the bike back," he answered smiling, "I thought if you'd pinched the money you'd hardly have left a side of bacon in the basket!"

I was only home for ten days when the *Empire McDermott* was ready to leave again for Montreal. As a regular member of the crew now I made my way to the Cornhill Shipping Office near Canning Place by the Pier Head and signed on. Our John was missing, having taken up a shore job, but Nutty was still there to keep an eye out for me. No doubt John had had a word with him.

The weather was quite friendly going out and when we got to Montreal it was like I'd never been away. Some of the lads had been on this run for several years but I was itching to see new places. I was very young and now that I'd been bitten by the 'sea bug' I wanted to see the world. I decided when I got home that as much and the St Lawrence River and Montreal had hypnotised me, I would look for another ship.

I'd been back in Liverpool for less than a fortnight when I was offered the *MV Derryheen* going to New York. Like my last ship, she had been a Royal Navy aircraft carrier called the *Empire McAndrew* but unlike the *McDermott* she had been completely refitted. The flight deck had been removed and her hangars properly converted for cargo. She was painted up in the McGowan-Cross colours of a black hull with a buff funnel displaying the letters MG in black. It was her maiden voyage as a cargo ship and to all intents and purposes, she was brand new.

I was on the twelve-four watch, but before we'd got very far we ran into a force ten gale. Just like the *McDermott* I was soon heaving for all I was worth. The difference this time was that the gale did not die down in a day. After three days I wanted to die. I made my mind up I would never set foot on a ship again. I would beg for my job back at the Co-Op. When I thought it was physically impossible to be sick again, I was sick again. I had never been so ill or totally miserable in my life. It was four days before the gale finally blew itself out. I was feeling pale, weak and very sorry for myself.

On watch I had been trying to persuade the Second Mate that I could handle the wheel. Now that the weather had eased, he decided to let me make a fool of myself. He was an easy-going chap who managed to drive everybody mad by whistling 'Sugar in the Morning, Sugar in the Evening' nearly every waking moment of the day and night. When he wasn't listening we called him 'Sugar'. He knew this was only my third trip but after only twenty minutes he also knew I could handle the wheel as well as any AB. Our John had taught me well.

My watch-mates were two Irish brothers, Frank and Peter McKinley. At four-bells Frank relieved me at the wheel. I told him how much wheel she was taking and went below. For the first time in more than four days I felt well enough to eat.

The following day the Bosun, Stan Hughes, a big man in his fifties came up to me.

"Right, Tommy," he said cheerfully, "now you're back in the land of the living, it's time for you to learn some seamanship. I want you to join up with old Ted Jones. There's a lot of splicing to be done, so you watch him carefully."

Old Ted was in his sixties and like most of the others had seen plenty of action during the war. After a couple of days with Ted I was beginning to get the hang of the basics, but I still had a lot to learn. We were twelve days out of Liverpool and twenty-four hours off New York. All the derricks were topped and the boards taken off the hatches in readiness for the longshoremen, as they called their dockers in New York.

The following day, we approached the Pilot Station and the ship's engines were put on 'Dead Slow Ahead'. The Third Mate gave the order for the Jacob's Ladder to go over the side. The Pilot came on board, a giant of a man wearing a bright flowered pink shirt and a baseball cap with a six inch peak smoking a cigar at least an inch longer. He might not turn too many heads today but in 1947 he looked like a Martian to me.

The engines were put on 'Full Ahead' and we made our way up the Hudson River, which had the same murky look about it as the Mersey. My first view of the Unites States of America was the Statue of Liberty and then the Empire State Building – both of which I recognised from magazine photographs. It was half-ten at night on June 20th when we tied up at Pier 56 on the west side of Manhatten.

Customs and Immigration Officers came on board. I found them more thorough than their Canadian counterparts. After being cleared we had to go back to work. There are many people who believe that once a ship hits port all hands hit town, but there was still work to be done for the crew on watch. The American dockers came on board, and compared to our lads back home they looked like they were going for a day out rather than going to work.

One of the lads called 'Sub-Up' and we made our way to the Chief Steward's cabin. I drew a sub of just over £2, but at over $4 to the pound sterling it came to $10. In the state of New York you had to be twenty-one to drink in the bars, so that was out for me and the other J.O.S.'s. There were older lads who chose not to drink. Eric Jones was saving up to get married after this trip and Paddy Bradford didn't smoke or touch drink at all. Another young fella was studying for his Officer's Ticket and spent all his spare time with his head in a book.

There was a funny incident a few days into our stay in New York. The ship had off-loaded her cargo and had gone across to a dry dock at Hobken for repairs to a leaking stern gland. Old Ted and a few of the hardened drinkers had gone through their cash and when they asked the Chief Steward for an additional sub he'd knocked them back. Ted then came up with the idea of going to the Blood Bank where they paid $5 for a pint of blood. Off they trooped, and after giving blood, they were each offered a glass of Port Wine which they took gladly. After relaxing for about ten minutes Ted approached the nurse.

"Thank you very much for the drink, but where do we pick up our five dollars?"

The nurse looked at him with a raised eyebrow.

"I'm afraid you've come to the wrong place." She said. "The Blood Bank you wanted is two blocks up. This is the Salvation Army, all our donors give their blood free!"

If there had been a rope handy Ted would have been strung up in Times Square there and then. On the same subject, I was once told that in the States you can earn three days remission off a prison sentence by giving a pint of blood.

The Seamen's Mission was well organised in New York. They came to the ship and organised a tour of the city, including a visit to the Statue of Liberty. Ted and his cronies agreed to come along on condition the old Padre laid on a bottle of Scotch Whisky and three or four cases of beer, but he'd been dealing with seamen for too long to fall for that.

The day after, a group of us were picked up by bus and with seamen from other ships we set off. A guide gave us a running comentary as we toured the city, pointing out City Hall, Radio City, Broadway and famous landmarks such as where well-known gangsters had been gunned down. The Statue of Liberty was located on Bedloe's Island near the city's Upper Bay. From 1830 to 1930 most of America's immigrants had arrived here and the statue carries a poem at its base. It read;

"Give me your tired
Your poor, your huddled masses
Yearning to breathe
Free the wretched refuse of your teeming shore
Send these, the homeless,
Tempest lost, to me
The Lamp beside the golden door."

We got back around midnight and when I told Ted the following morning, he reckoned I'd seen more of New York in one day than he had in twenty years! All Ted ever did in port was spend his sub in the local bars. He knew very little about the dozens of cities he'd been to, but if you asked him about the bars and taverns of the world, he was an expert!

Stan the Bosun came into the Mess Room looking none to pleased.

"Well, lads, we've been well and truly Shanghaid!"

All hands looked at him.

"We're not going back to Liverpool," he went on, "we've

received orders for New Zealand!"

There was a mixed reaction. Most of the lads were fairly cheesed off as the trip would now last several months instead of a few weeks. Personally, I was made up. I was just getting used to the excitement of New York after the beauty of Canada and now I was going 'down under'. There was much muttering and moaning, but then a voice piped up from the corner.

"I don't know what yer've all got to complain about." It was Eric Jones. "I've got to cancel me bloody wedding!"

Chapter 7
The Panama Canal

We left New York on July 2nd bound for Auckland. At a steady nine knots it took about four days to reach Panama. There was a lot of work to be done and I was becoming fairly proficient at knots and splices. The standard of seamanship was very high among the AB's but old Ted just seemed to have that bit extra. It was a rough crossing, running south on the Atlantic towards the West Indies, but the last storm had sorted me out. I was never sea-sick again. We passed through the Windward Passage that separates Cuba and Haiti and then crossed the Caribbean Sea to Panama.

The Bosun approached the Peggy and myself.

"Right, lads, between now and the Panama Canal I want you to collect as much bread as you can."

The pair of us looked at each other and then at the Bosun as if he'd gone off his trolley.

"What for?" we asked him.

"OK," he said, "it's your first trip this way so you can't be expected to know. When we get to the Canal they use mules instead of tugs to help pull the ships through the locks. They're not the best fed animals in the world so we do what we can to help."

Blimey, I thought, mules pulling a ship of this size – there must be bloomin' hundreds of them!

Anyway, four days later we arrived at Colon, the northern entrance to the Canal and we'd managed to scavenge two sacks full of bread. There were about ten ships laying at anchor waiting to enter the Canal in convoy. At about mid-day we began to move forward in the line. At the first lock, named Catun, me and the Peggy spotted the mules we'd been scraping together bread for. We'd both fallen for it alright! The mules were small, but very powerful electric locomotives. We had one each on the starboard bow and quarter and the same on the port side. A couple of the lads were giving us a bit of stick as we threw the bread for the birds.

The Third Officer had been up and down the Canal several times and he told us about the mules, the locks and a lot of the background of the Panama Canal. It had cost the Americans the best part of $400 million to build and took thirty-two years, opening in 1914. It was forty-two miles long with channels giving access to the Pacific and Atlantic Oceans. The minimum depth was forty-two feet

We entered the Canal at Colon and were raised in three stages to eighty-five feet above sea-level through the Gatun Locks and back down to sea-level and the Pacific Ocean at the Miraflores Locks at Balboa. One of the fascinating sights on the Canal was when passing through the Celebra Cut, so narrow it was almost possible to touch the walls from the ship's rails. Making steady progress, I was drawn to a copper plate set in the wall. On it were two workmen with shovels as a tribute to the men who had died in the thirty-two years it had taken to build the Canal. According to our Third Officer, forty-thousand men lost their lives in its construction, but as that was about two-dozen men every single week, I decided he'd probably added a couple of thousand each time he told the story.

Passing the port of Panama we entered the Pacific and were three weeks from Auckland. I saw porpoises for the first time in my young life, five feet long with blunt, rounded snouts, and an albatros – one of the largest seabirds in the world with huge grey wings and a white body. The albatros could range the high-seas for months without ever seeing land. The cook came up on deck and threw the contents of the 'rosey', a bin for waste food, over the ship's side and within minutes sharks appeared. Old Ted pointed one out.

"That's a Grey Nurse!" he said, "one of the most vicious sharks in the world!"

And they looked it too.

A week out of Panama we were forced to stop to change a damaged piston which took about four hours. When we finally got going again the sharks stayed with us for a while awaiting more easy pickings, but eventually they disappeared from view.

There was plenty of work to do on deck to keep us occupied and below, most of the crew had a hobby of some kind. A few of the lads liked to mount model ships inside bottles, others carved sailing ships out of chicken breast bones. My hobby became knots and splicing and my tutor, of course, was old Ted.

All hands, including Deck Boys, were allowed two cans of beer a day and I was happy to give my allowance to Ted. If nothing else, this made him pretty keen to patiently answer all my questions about knots and splices. To protect his supply he promised to show me how to make cargo nets and do wire splicing. I got the hang of the nets easily enough, but wire splicing was an art form.

"The easiest splice," Ted said, "is the Liverpool Splice, but the Aussies and the Kiwis won't use it."

"Why not?" I asked.

"A few years ago there was a bad accident down there. A couple of fellas were killed and they blamed it on the Liverpool Splice. They use a locking splice now."

The Liverpool Splice was not a locking splice and any Boy Scout could learn it in twenty minutes. The Australian Locking Splice was much more difficult, but as all our rigging was brand new we didn't have to worry about it.

We were getting closer to New Zealand and you could tell. The lads were shaving their beards or pressing their 'go ashores' as they called them. The subject of girls became more popular as some of the lads talked about 'conquests' made on previous visits.

At nine-thirty on August 31st we arrived in Waitman Harbour, Aukland, the largest city and main seaport in New Zealand. The ship was tied up and the gangway lowered. The ship's agent came on board and few men were held in higher regard by the crew. He carried the document for where the ship was going next, but far more important to us he brought the mail from home and money for the lads to go ashore. An hour after we'd tied up, the dockers came on board and started work. Like the Americans they were much smarter dressed than our lads back home. I often wondered what American and Australasian sailors made of the dockers when they sailed into Liverpool.

The Bosun came in with a sackful of mail. I wasn't much of a letter-writer and consequently didn't get much post.

"Half and hour," he said, "Sub-Up!"

I drew £10. Ted and his boozing mates drew £30 or even £40 but as most of them were single they could afford it. The Bosun came up to me.

"Right, young Dusty. I'm going to give you job and finish." which meant when I was done my time was my own. "Go to the wheel-house and clean up all the brass."

I knew well enough that the wheel-house was like a brass foundry! I was just about to start when the Captain came in.

"I would rather you left that, young man," he said, "I have friends due."

Thank God for that, I thought, and reported back to the

Bosun.

"That'll do today then, but make sure you get it done tomorrow," he said.

★ ★ ★ ★

It was half-five and with the Peggy, the Galley Boy and the Pantry Boy we had dinner on board and then got into out Yankee posing gear and set off to find a dance hall. Walking up Queen's Street I noticed a lot of people carrying brown paper bags, which I found out later were 'carry-outs', full of bottled beer because the pubs closed at six o'clock. We found a dance hall, had a fine time and got back to the *Derryheen* about midnight.

Back on board, Ted and his cronies were singing their heads off in the Mess Room. One lad was singing 'Kevin Barry', an old Irish Nationalist song and Ted had a go at 'Maggie May'. Geordie, who you couldn't understand head nor tail of at the best of times, was drunkenly reciting poetry. It was about then the fight broke out.

Ronnie McGee, a donkey greaser, shouted over to Geordie, who was actually from West Hartlepool.

"Hey, Geordie! Who hanged the monkey then?"

For the benefit of all those who haven't heard this much told story ... During the Napoleonic wars, a monkey, probably having fell overboard from a passing ship, was discovered on the beach at Hartlepool. Fearing an invasion from the French, local people, in a wave of paranoia and hysteria, hanged the monkey as a spy. The town of Hartlepool is still living this bizarre, but true episode down to this day.

Anyway, the next thing, there was crockery and beer-bottles flying all over the Mess. Geordie launched himself at McGee, taking a table and a couple of AB's with him. The bulkheads were decorated in brown sauce and ketchup and while all this was going on, old Ted kept on singing ...

"...for the judge he guilty found her,
Of robbing a homeward bounder,
That dirty, robbing, no-good Maggie May!
Oh, Maggie, Maggie May ..."

Those who had managed to get to sleep were now wide awake and before long the Chief Officer and the Bosun came bounding in.

"OK, you piss 'eads, break it up!"

Everything quietened down pretty quickly, except for Ted ...

"...they have taken her away,
And she'll never walk down
Lime Street any ..."

"Shut up!"

Ted finally shut up. The Bosun looked at the disaster-area around him.

"Everybody to their bunks, we'll sort this out in the morning when you're all sober."

The following morning, it was left to the Peggy and me to clear up the debris. It took us over an hour and when we finally sat down to breakfast, Ted came in looking for a beer as a 'curer'. He was followed by Ronnie McGee, Gerry Brown and Billy Dunne with the same idea, but they had to settle for a cup of tea. Those who weren't party to the trouble were less than pleased at the state of the Mess. One of the ABs, Bill Bowers, a big man, turned on Ted.

"If this happens again, you and your pissed-up mates will be having your food on the deck."

"And who the bleedin' 'ell are you?"

Another slanging match was gathering momentum when the Bosun came in.

"You four on the Bridge at ten o'clock." Nobody was in any doubt as to the four he was referring to, though surprisingly, Geordie was left alone. The Ship's Master was Captain Storme, an appropriate name for a 'skipper', but not for this man. He was only about five-feet-five and more like a priest or parson. He was mild-mannered, but very professional and tolerated no messing about. Apparently he came straight to the point.

"If I hear of any more trouble from any of you, I'll stop your tap," which meant no more beer at sea and no more 'subs' in port. This was the stiffest punishment he could have dished out to them, not least old Ted.

"You will pay for the damaged crockery and I don't expect to see you up here again."

Ted was about to say something in his defence when the Captain cut him short.

"That will be all, leave the Bridge!"

When they came back to the Mess, they each had a good moan, swearing and cursing, except for Ted who was thinking quietly to himself. He hadn't started the fighting and took no part in it. He'd been tarred with the same brush as his mates and as there were probably few things in life as important to Ted as his 'tap' he took the old man's words very seriously. From that moment he began to drift away from McGee, Brown and Dunne.

We'd been a week in Auckland off-loading our cargo, which was all kinds of everything, including, funnily enough, kitchen sinks. There was a shortage of labour generally in New Zealand. The Auckland dockers would work until the job was done, even if it was the early hours of the morning, and when we'd finished our shift we were asked to muck in. I wasn't very happy about this and although I wasn't about to refuse, I let Ted know how I felt.

"What are you talking about?" he said.

"Well, it's not our fault there's not enough dockers, and we work hard enough on our watch. It just doesn't seem fair."

"Oh, you silly sod!" Ted laughed. "You don't do it for nothing! These fellas are earning about four or five times as much as you and when you're working with them you get paid the same money!"

"The same money!" I gasped. "Those fellas are on about seven quid a week!"

"I know they are." Said Ted. "So if you put in a few hours after each shift you've got yourself an easy couple of quid."

Before Ted had finished I'd jumped up and was on my way out of the Mess. This kind of overtime I could live with!

Chapter 8
A Double Jump!

Working with the dockers, I noticed that keenest to do the extra work were the younger lads like myself who didn't earn very much. We had four Bridge Cadets who were paid a pittance and they were prepared to work every hour God sent. Generally, they stayed away from the rest of the crew so I never got to know them very well, but they had a right reputation when thy went ashore. Hardly the country's best ambassadors, they caused trouble wherever they went, but they were only young and worked long hours so maybe this was their way of letting off steam.

The extra work meant extra cash and we were all making the most of it. The Seamen's Mission invited the crew to a performance of Maori singing and dancing. Much to our surprise, Ted's former drinking pals joined us. The Mission provided the transport and getting on the bus, McGee said, "Thought we might as well join the Mission Bums."

He was referring to me and my mates who didn't drink and

only wanted to go on tours or to dances and the Mission laid all this on. McGee, Brown and Dunne already had a few beers under their belt and were starting to annoy a few of the other passengers. One big bloke, off another ship, got up and walked over to McGee who was doing most of the shouting.

"I hope you weren't referring to me with your comment about Mission Bums?"

McGee went pale and said, "Of course not, just having a joke with our shipmates," pointing over at us.

The Maoris were wonderful. I was fascinated by their chants, songs and dances, which are now famous the world over with the pre-match ritual of the All-Blacks rugby team. The songs I remember were 'On the road to Toacua', 'You are my only Treasure' and 'He's gone away to the island of Tahiti'.

As we were leaving, McGee and company were well-oiled and trying to copy the Maori dancing. It all seemed to be in good fun and we left them to it, getting back to the ship just after midnight. The 'boozers' got back about an hour later by taxi, costing them a small fortune and three of them had a right old ding-dong the following morning, blaming the other for missing the bus.

Apparently, Dunne had fallen in love with one of the Maori girls and when she gave him a big smile and a friendly kiss he thought this qualified as a 'yes' to a marriage proposal. Things got out of hand and finally a six-foot-six Maori gave him a solid punch on the nose. There was blood everywhere and when he finally came round, McGee and Brown were in two minds about taking him back to the ship or off to hospital. They tried to draw

Ted in to referee the argument, but he kept out of it. He was sitting on a hatch, splicing a rope and smoking a pipe, no doubt noting the wisdom of distancing himself from the three of them.

★ ★ ★ ★

On Saturday we finished particularly early, so Paul – the Officers Steward, Joe – the Pantry Boy, Eric – the Galley Boy and me decided to go ashore. With plenty of time to kill we took a walk along the docks. Paul knew his ships and pointed out the different shipping companies represented by the vessels in port; The Blue Star Line, The Post Line, The Larrinaga Line, The Bank Line, The Ropner Line and the Shaw Savill Line, one of the most famous Liverpool companies.

Just docking at the time was the *MV Rangitiki*, 16,000.698 tons, of The Federal Line and belonging to New Zealand Shipping Company. As the saying goes, she was 'down to the gunwhale' full of immigrants from all over Europe. Due to the shortage of labour the New Zealand Government encouraged the new arrivals and I knew of the £10 assisted passage from the UK.

There was another Federal Line ship off-loading passengers, the 'SS Ruahine'. It was a mass migration of people running away from their own countries hoping to better their lives. For many it worked out very well, but others just brought their real problems with them. Personally, I liked New Zealand but I didn't think I could settle there. I still got home-sick from time to time.

After twelve days we were ready to leave for Wellington, the country's capital at the southern tip of North Island on the Cook Strait. The day we were leaving, flying the Blue Peter, one of the

ABs, Henry, was acting oddly, going ashore four or five times carrying a paper bag. A few of the lads were wondering what he was pinching, but finally he never came back. Henry had jumped ships just two hours before we sailed. The Bosun came round checking everybody was aboard and had to report to the Chief Officer that there was an AB missing. There was no time to wait for him to turn up or be replaced, so we set off one AB adrift and a cadet standing in for him.

★ ★ ★ ★

We arived at Wellington in a few days and made ready for the dockers to start work. No sooner than they were on board when the wind got up and it started pouring with rain. We had a hell of a job securing the hatch covers.

Old Ted said, "Now you know why it's called Windy Wellington!"

The weather was dreadful and it was four days before the dockers came back. I found Wellington to be a very quiet city, hardly a capital at all. Mind you, having never been to London I thought Liverpool should have been the capital of England, so who was I to say? Like Liverpool though, the people were very friendly.

We weren't due to stay in Wellington very long, and with Eric and Joe we took an opportunity one night to go ashore, where we found a very nice dance hall. We had a good night and afterwards were invited to a party. It was quite amazing, but it seemed nearly everybody could play a musical instrument, mostly ukeles, banjoes and accordions.

I was approached by a young Maori.

"Get that down yer, mate, it'll put hairs on yer chest!"

"No thanks." I said. "I'll just have a lemonade."

He looked astounded. "What's lemonade?"

From that day to this I have no recollection of getting back to the ship. Whatever I drank that night I wouldn't mind a few pints of today! That was my first booze-up and the following day I swore it would be my last. It was a full week before I felt right.

★ ★ ★ ★

The day before we sailed, a new AB joined the ship to take Henry's place. His name was Harry.

"Just call me H!" He said, so H it was. He was well into his sixties, a big man and fit for his age. His accent was a mixture of cockney and Kiwi. He'd been living on the New Zealand coast for years, but wanted to go home to London for a while and see his family. The *Derryheen* was docking in London when she got back to England, so this was ideal.

We waved farewell to our new-found friends on the quayside and set sail for Dunedin, further down the coast on South Island, with a part cargo. We were having breakfast when McGee walked into the Mess. Since leaving Liverpool he'd sat at the same seat for every meal and as he seemed quite obsessed with this the lads humoured him left his place alone. He came in, his usual 'cheerful' self, snarling at the least thing, to find H sitting in hs chair. He glared at him.

"You're sitting in my chair!"

H looked up briefly, then calmly went back to his meal before answering.

"When you joined the ship did you bring this chair with you?"

For a moment McGee was lost for words.

"You bleedin' half-baked Kiwi!" he screamed. But H didn't bite. He answered calmly.

"You're the first Scouser I've ever met who didn't have any brains." He stood up slowly. "If you want your chair back you'll have to fight for it!"

Dunne and Brown were egging McGee on. H looked at the three of them in turn.

"I've been on this ship three days and I've listened to you three gasbag know-it-alls enough. So I'll tell you what I'll do. One at a time I'll take you up on deck and knock some sense into you. If you feel better about it, I'll take the three of you at the same time. What's it to be?"

Dunne was the first to answer. "Not on board ship, we've trouble enough with the old man. We'll sort it out in Dunedin."

"OK, please yourself." Said H, sitting down again in the same place.

★ ★ ★ ★

On Monday 16th September, just before noon, we arrived at Dunedin. The dockers came on board but for once they were in no hurry and didn't make a start for a couple of hours. Stan, the Bosun said they were on a 'go-slow' and to leave them be.

"They're looking for the slightest excuse to walk off, so no stupid, sarcy comments or we'll be stuck here for weeks!"

Nobody liked Dunedin that much, so nothing was said. All the dockers seemed to know H.

"Any problems?" one said to him.

"Nothing I can't handle, thanks, Bill."

Dunne just happened to be walking past and heard this. Both Dunne and Brown had laid of H but McGee had been humiliated by him and was determined to get even. The following day one of the dockers called McGee over.

"I've heard you and H don't hit it off together."

"What the bleedin' 'ell's it got to do with you!"

The docker stood toe-to-toe with McGee and stared at him hard.

"If I hear you've given H any more problems, take it from me, you won't be seeing the old country again."

"You'll need an army if you fancy your chances!"

"Take a look behind me, sunshine."

McGee looked up and about twenty yards away stood about a dozen large, gruesome looking dockers. He had a face like thunder but stormed off and never bothered H again after that.

We docked at each of the New Zealand ports and then headed for Savu on the Fiji Islands for sugar. We did a few Australasian ports, my favourite being Geelong in Port Philip Bay near Melbourne, and Townsville in the North-East behind the Great

Barrier Reef. If ever I were to settle in Australia, it would be in Geelong or Townsville.

It was in Townsville that H jumped ship, never to be seen again, so McGee got his chair back after all. It turned out later that H had no intention of going back to 'Blighty' to see his relatives. He made a living out of jumping aboard short-handed foreign ships along the coats of New Zealand and Australia and jumping off again before they headed home. As losing ABs was a regular occurrence in this part of the world, he was never short of work.

Apparently, H was a staunch Trade Unionist and his political views were well known with the local authorities. He'd caused a lot of trouble in the past and had been banned by the Union Steam Ship Company that belonged to the New Zealand Merchant Service. If he wasn't much liked by the bosses, he was very popular with the dockers, which was why McGee had had the trouble in Dunedin.

He spent his life hopping around the Australasian ports, no doubt spreading his political gospel where he could. When his ship was going abroad he would use the line that he wanted to buy presents for relatives back home and draw as much of his wages as he could. Then he'd disappear.

Obviously, the Chief Steward would be taken in by him or he wouldn't have been allowed to 'sub' anything, but he was good at his job and very plausible.

"He was a character and a half, wasn't he!" Ted said.

"I thought he was alright." I replied.

"I thought he was alright, too," added Ted, "certainly put the wind up McGee. Must say though, it's the first time I've known a fella to jump on a ship and then jump off again like that and not tell a soul what he's up to."

"Like a double jump!" I said.

"That's one way of putting it." he said, tugging on his pipe.

★ ★ ★ ★

Stan was complaining about severe pains in his left leg and went to see the shore doctor who had him hospitalised. Frank McInley was promoted to Bosun for the homeward voyage. We came home via the Suez Canal and old Ted gave me a slap on the shoulder.

"When you get back to England, Tommy, you'll have done it!"

"Done what?"

"Circumnavigated the globe! You left the Atlantic travelling west and came back to it still travelling west. When you get home, Tommy, you can tell your mam you've been around the world. And you'll be telling the truth!"

"Wow!"

It was difficult for a lad barely seventeen to take it in. We headed north-west across the Indian Ocean and it was at that time when Christmas came. It was my first Christmas away from home and I missed everyone badly. Most of the lads would rather have been somewhere else, but generally they made the most of it. The tradition on most ships was for the Chief Officer, Chief Engineer and the other Officers to serve the crew with Christmas dinner and the *Derryheen* was no exception. It was all good fun.

On New Year's Eve, the tradition at midnight, the usual eight bells are rung twice. Eight 'ringing out the old' and eight 'ringing in the new'. As it was my first New Year at sea and I was on the Watch at the time, I was given the honour and I was quite chuffed to do it.

★ ★ ★ ★

The trip had lasted nine and a half months. I'd been around the world and 'down under' by the time we finally docked in London on the 19th March 1948, the first time I'd been there.

"This is your first visit to London, then Tommy?" Frank asked.

"Yeah!"

"I can think of a couple of quicker ways of getting here than the way you've just come!"

Chapter 9
North v South

We were paid off the same day and I picked up £96, probably more than a couple of thousand quid in today's money. Most of the lads were staying the night in London and tried to persuade me to do the same. They'd been there before and knew their way around, talking about the fancy clubs they'd be going to. In the end I decided against it. I was very homesick and got the first train back to Liverpool, but it was Ted who had finally made my mind up for me.

"You get off home, lad," he said, "you've a lot of money on you and this is a big city for a young fella. The girls in these clubs will have that money off you in minutes."

On the train I was in a compartment with four other seamen who'd been paid off another ship after being away for more than eighteen months. They invited me to join them in a game of poker.

"No, thanks," I said, "I only play crib." And it proved to be a wise move. Before we got to Lime Street one of them had lost all but a few pounds of his pay-off. I could sense trouble brewing so I took my gear off the rack and moved to another carriage. I'd no sooner gone than all hell broke loose. There were accusations of cheating, fists flying and money all over the place.

"I've been away for a bloody year and a half!" said the lad who'd lost his money, "and I've barely got the bloody taxi fare home!"

★ ★ ★ ★

It was little more than a year since I first set sail on the *Empire McDermott*, but already I'd been to Canada, the US, and around the world via the Panama Canal, New Zealand, Australia, the Fiji Isles, the Suez Canal and the Mediterranean Sea. I was hungry to see more of the world and three weeks after I'd docked in London I signed up with Thos & Jas Harrison ship, the *SS Inventor*, bound for the West Indies and the Gulf of Mexico.

She was a big ship at 9,298 tons and a coal burner. We sailed from Brunswick Dock on the 10th April and within days I knew she was a bad ship. Most of the firemen came from the south of Liverpool and most of the deck crew were northenders. I've no idea why, but in those days there was a lot of rivalry between the two. It might have been something to do with religion because the north end was predominantly Irish Catholic, but personally I never got caught up in it.

Our first stop was Port of Spain, Trinidad and there had already been three of four fights by the time we got there. The food was dreadful and I was glad to get ashore and have a decent meal in peace. The Harrison ships carried funnel markings of two 'fat' bands and one 'lean', which were remarkably similar to the bacon we were served twice a week. On each rasher there was a 'pencil' of lean bacon running through a piece of fat. We were also fed what was known as 'Board of Trade Salad', which was corned beef mixed with beetroot and sliced onions. Generally, the grub was very basic.

Trinidad was a lot of fun and very friendly, as long as you kept out of the way of the clashes between our crew each time they came across each other. We off-loaded our cargo which included railway lines and took on sugar and rum. Our next port of call was Caracas in Venezuala, four hundred miles west across the Lesser Antilles of the Caribbean Sea. After a short stay we moved on to Willemstad on the Island of Curacao. We were due to stay there for just two days but we'd developed engine trouble and were told we'd be there for at least a week.

Those who had sufficient funds 'in the ship' were allowed to draw a sub, but those who didn't had to do without. Usually, seamen would help each other out in these situations, but that was never going to happen on the *Inventor*. I have to say that 'broaching' of the cargo was rife on the ship, so there wasn't a problem with cash for the crew deck. When the sailors were togged up and going ashore and the firemen were stuck aboard, the atmosphere was very hostile, to say the least.

Curacao is a beautiful island and most of the lads were happy spending their time on the beach at Happy Valley. From Willemstad we sailed north-west about five hundred miles or more across the Caribbean to Kingston, Jamaica. There, we off-loaded more of the cargo and took on more sugar. During our stop in Kingston, the crew were invited to the Rum Brewery which was a fascinating tour. For the lads who were short of cash it was an opportunity for a good 'piss-up'. As we left we were each given two free bottles of rum as a gift, and going back to the ship I feared the worst.

As it happened, the rum cheered everybody up and the sailors and firemen put their differences to one side and decided to return to the ship for a party. One by one they staggered up the gangway, each clutching their two bottles as if their life depended on it. From the wing of the ship's Bridge, the Captain, a distinguished looking grey-haired man from the Orkneys, watched the performance. He called out below to the Third Officer, a man no bigger that five feet six and weighed eight stone.

"As those men come aboard, Third Mate, I want you to confiscate those bottles and throw them over the side!"

"Yes, sir!" answered the Mate standing at the top of the gangway, looking pompous and very pleased with himself. The first seaman up the gangway was 'Smile-a-While' Henry Mulrooney, who didn't have a tooth in his head. He had a head and neck like a bull terrier, but perhaps wasn't as good-looking! The Officer raised his hands to Henry and, in his 'posh' southern accent said, "Hand those bottles over to me at once!" In a way a school teacher might address a seven year old.

Henry glared at him. "Get out of my way!"

The Officer stood his ground for a moment but Henry took a run at him and he was off like a shot. Henry looked up at the Captain. "Why don't you come down and take them off me?"

The Chief Engineer was nearby leaning over the ship's rail. On another ship, he would have stepped in and put a stop to the insubordination, but there was no love lost between him and the old man either, so he ignored the whole thing. To add to this, most of the men boarding the ship who were enjoying themselves, were his firemen and they hadn't had too much fun on this trip so far.

He knew how they had worked down below in temperatures in excess of one hundred and twenty degrees and they were long overdue in letting off a bit of steam. The Captain and his officers never ventured down the stock hole where the men had to piss of the palms of their hands to ease the pain of blisters, or take a 'crap' on the coal because there was no time to do it any other way. He never saw them dragging sacks full of cinders up through the Fiddle and on to the deck to throw them over the side. The Chief Engineer did. He was as hard as any of his firemen and would fight any of them if he had to, but he respected each and every one of them. The Officers had their meals in the Saloon, but he preferred to eat in his cabin even though the old man had voiced his objections.

The party took place without incident and a day or so later we set off for the Gulf of Mexico, passing through the Yucatan Channel that separates Mexico and Cuba. We called at Veracruz (Mexico), Galveston (Texas) and New Orleans (Louisiana). We spent a few days in each port and I was overwhelmed by them. I wanted to live in Galveston, then I wanted to live in New Orleans. They are wonderful cities with wonderful people. I was determined that one day I would live there, but it was very odd how homeward bound, the feeling quickly faded as I got nearer and nearer to Liverpool. I might wander all over the world but I would only ever have one home.

We got down to overhauling the ship's gear – painting the masts, the bulkheads, deckheads, and of course, the funnel, two 'fat' and one 'lean'. As we got nearer home she was beginning to look like a real lady, her deck housing was a brilliant white. The Chief Officer was on the wing of the Bridge, admiring his ship and thinking to himself how impressed the company Superintendent would be when we got back to Liverpool. The paint was still wet and would be for a few hours, but she looked very impressive.

It was just then occurred an incident which for me summed up the whole voyage. Without giving the notice he would have done normally, the Chief Engineer decided to blow the Boiler Tubes. From the funnel came an enormous belch of thick black smoke. The Chief Officer looked on in horrified anguish. He could not believe his eyes as the dense soot caked over his immaculate paintwork. He lost complete control of himself and challenged the Chief Engineer to a fight on deck.

"You bastard! You complete and utter bastard! I'll kill you! May God strike me down if I don't kill you!"

The Chief Engineer was delighted. "Oh, piss off, sunshine!" he said with a smirk on his face.

Within a few seconds the old man turned up and put a stop to it, dragging his Chief Officer away still spitting and frothing. As they disappeared the Chief Engineer's smirk turned into the broadest grin and he laughed heartily as any man I've ever heard.

"My God!" he spluttered, "two months of crap and worth every bleedin' minute just for that!"

Word soon spread to the other firemen below and the world was right with them too.

Normally, the Engineer would ring the Bridge before he blew the tubes and the Officer there would bring the ship into the wind or, probably on this occasion, ask him to wait a few hours. We couldn't wash the paint down because it was still wet and we couldn't paint it again because we'd done such a thorough job we had very little paint left. We came down the Mersey looking like an old tramp ship that hadn't been painted since the day she was launched. We tied up at the quayside and there was the Superintendent looking up at the ship, looking far from happy.

The following day we were paid off at Cornhill and I knew I wouldn't be going out with her again. During my life at sea, if there was one ship I was glad to see the back of, it was the *S.S. Inventor*.

Chapter 10
The Foo-Foo Boys

I'd been home for three weeks when I reported to the Seaman's Pool. I handed my discharge book to the same clerk who had offered me the *Derryheen*, 'Shanghai' Griffiths. Most of the shipping clerks hadn't been to sea but they looked the part in their uniforms. There was more gold braid in the Pool than there was on the Ark Royal! Shangai had two gold braids equal to a Second Officer on a merchant ship and most of the lads were against it. Nobody believed the clerks worked as hard as a ship's Officer to wear those gold braids.

"I have a nice little job for you," said Shangai. "It's a six week trip on a Cunard ship, the *Fort Musquarano*.

The last time I had been given 'a nice little job' by Shanghai I disappeared for nearly a year!

"She's laying off the Huskisson Dock and sails for New York on Wednesday."

The following day, 5th July 1948 I signed on at Cornhill. Most of the men were into the company for an 'Advance Note' which could be cashed with a money-lender for a charge of 1s.6d in the pound. The 'Note' was supposed to be to buy working gear or to give the wife a few bob before sailing. In practice, the money was usually spent on a giant bender before sailing. A lender by the name of Whitfield was known to most of the lads. Three days after the ship sailed he could take the notes to the Pool and be paid, but they were worthless if the seaman missed his ship. The lender was resented by nearly everyone because of th money he made doing nothing. If he ever lost out that was regarded as his hard luck, or so most seamen thought, but that is another tale.

On the 7th, we were on stand-by for sailing and the Bosun reported to the Chief Officer that no fewer than three ABs were adrift. The donkeyman reported that he was four firemen light.

The Captain called out to the Chief Officer. "Mr Mate, if those men are not on board in twenty minutes I will sail without them. We'll anchor in the River and pick up the necessary men tomorrow."

"I think I know where they might be, sir," the Bosun said.

"I think I do too, sir!" said the donkeyman.

They both left the ship and walked across to one of the pubs on the Dock Road, 'Broken Nose Jacks'. They went inside and good enough, the seven missing seafarers were there without a care in the world, singing their heads off. The sailors were in one corner and the firemen in the other. The Bosun went over to the three ABs.

"You've got five minutes to sup-up that ale and get on board or we sail without you!"

The donkeyman said much the same. "Come on! Five minutes or you can take as long as you like!"

They all called the pair fit to burn but eventually they staggered to their feet and made their way out of the pub and across to the ship. The gangway was brought in straight away and we set sail fro New York.

★ ★ ★ ★

Four days out of Liverpool we ran into a Force Eight gale and the cargo in the N°1 hold shifted. All hands were wanted down the hold and when I got there two tractors had come adrift. The Captain ordered the ship to 'Hove-To', and it took four hours to secure the cargo and make it safe. The blame was put squarely on the shore gang who had lashed the cargo. The Bosun made no secret of his contempt for them.

"Boy Scouts could have done a bloody better job."

The shore gangs were the 'cowboys' of the docks. Certain standards had to be kept to hold onto your job as a seaman or a docker, but anybody could be taken on in the shore gangs. Mostly they were used by the dockers or seamen who had to get off for a wedding or funeral and needed somebody to stand in. One company, Alfred Holt, who owned The Blue Funnel Line, insisted that the proper papers be produced by every single person who came aboard their ships. They were the exception. There were a lot of shore gangs about and though they may have been first-class soldiers during the war they knew little about seamanship. Once the cargo was made safe the old man expertly brought the ship about and put her back on her original course.

Most of our firemen were from the Scotland Road area, and take my word for it, they were real tough nuts. They had a tough job to do, too. Two of them, 'Big Paddy' McLoughlin and 'Shoulders' McLean had each brought a son on board for their first trip working as trimmers. 'Shoulders' was only five-feet-five inches tall, but he must have been six feet wide. He was a very strong man, to say the least. I was on the twelve-four Watch and my two mates were 'Monkey' Williams and 'Fat' Byrnes. 'Monkey' deserved his name, I've never seen a man take so many chances as he did up a mast.

'Fat' Byrnes was not fat because of what he ate, but because of gland problems. Despite his size he was surprisingly agile and it didn't seem to bother him being called 'Fat'. His real name was Paul and he was a likeable bloke who was difficult to upset. The boy seamen like me, showed him some respect by calling him Paul. Like 'Nutty' on the *Empire McDermott*, Paul was invited to take a lower bunk by his cabin mates. He was a popular lad, but not that popular!

I came off Watch at four o'clocks and, out of curiosity, decided to have a 'nose' down the stock hole. 'Shoulders' was teaching his son the tricks of the trade. There was a mountain of coal and placed on a lower mound was a twenty foot plank. The trimmer would push his wheelbarrow to the base of the mound, turn it around and fill it with coal until it overflowed. The ship was only rolling slightly but was pitching every few seconds.

"Right!" said 'Shoulders', "wait for the next pitch then go!"

The fireman was waiting for his coal like a bricklayer waiting for his hod carrier. The young fella got his timing right and ran down the plank and tipped his load at the fireman's feet. Once or twice he missed the pitching of the ship and spilt his load before he got to the end of the plank. Then he just ran back and started again. You could see tears in his eyes and blisters on his hands. He wore a cap that was too big for him and kept slipping over his eyes. He wore heavy bib-and-brace overalls and a sweat rag round his neck. His hob-nail boots looked about three sizes too big. Yet he never complained or cried out, he just got on with the job.

One thing I noticed about firemen and trimmers was that they all wore the buckle of their belts back to front. One of the older lads tried to pull the wool over my eyes saying there was only one shop in Liverpool that sold that kind of belt. In fact, the firemen turned their belts around because working in front of the ship's fires for hours on end meant the buckle became red-hot.

I climbed into my bunk ready for a good sleep. The ship was beginning to roll around a fair but my sea-sick days were over. I was thinking about the young trimmer down below, running up and down that plank for four hours at a time. Thank God, I'm on deck, I thought. Some days it got very cold, especially on the North Atlantic run, but I wouldn't swap it.

About a week out of Liverpool the weather improved and we spent our time on deck overhauling the lifting gear and doing a spot of painting and cleaning. As the weather got better so did everyone's mood. There was a lot of singing and joking and we all got to know each other better. I've got very fond memories of those sunny days on deck. There was a lot of talent among the crew and they formed what they called 'The Foo Foo Band'. 'Red' Donelly was on the bass, which was a tea-chest and a brush handle with a thin cord running the length of the handle. It was amazing the notes he could play. 'Shoulders' McLean was on the clappers; 'Monkey' Williams on the accordion and 'Paddy' Darkin, a J.O.S., on the harmonica.

Each weekend and a few evenings when the mood was right the band would play and we'd have a good old sing-song. The two first-trip trimmers were finding their sea-legs and started to join in. Most of the crew would give a song in turn when called on. A few were very good but others would frighten the living daylights out of the ship's cat!

Frank Whittaker, as a boy, had been going to sea when there were sailing-ships. He would never tell anybody how old he was, but we reckon he was about a hundred and twenty! He had a marvellous head of hair, silver-grey and bobtailed. He wouldn't give a song, but didn't need asking twice to recite one of his famous poems. He stood in the middle of the Mess and off he went ...

> "Pipe all hands to man the capstan,
> See your cables running clear,
> For when we've weighed our anchor,
> To Australia's shores we'll steer."

It might have been easy enough to get Frank started but it was the devil's own job to get him to stop!

"Now listen, all ye landsmen,
To what we've got to say,
Around Cape Horn and home again,
That was the sailor's way."

Before he had a chance to get into the next verse or the next poem The Foo Foo Band started playing. The problem with Frank's poems was nobody was really sure where one finished and the next one started. It didn't seem to matter.

"Ladies and Gentlemen!" shouted 'Shoulders'.

"What ladies?" Big Paddy replied.

"I'll have one!" said Paul.

"I'll have two!" said Monkey.

"Shut up! Shut up!" 'Shoulders' shouted again. "Let me introduce you to our next artist this evening, a big round of applause please for our ever popular 'Pongo' Waring!".

"Booo! Booo!"

'Pongo' gave a rendition of 'When my old Wedding Ring was New" but it was murderous. About half-way through, to everyone's relief, he forgot the words.

"Thank God for that!"

"Jesus, Pongo! Sit down!"

"Gag him, quick!"

Pongo sat down, not pleased. He'd earned his nick-name, he was one of those sailors who took a shower every three months whether he needed one or not! Nights such as this were plentiful and good fun.

A week later, we came upon the US coastline, cruising past Long Island into New York. The two young trimmers came up on deck and stood goggle-eyed at the Statue of Liberty, the Empire State Building and all the other skyscrapers that came into view – pretty much as I had done a year earlier. We docked at Pier 92 and almost immediately the dockers were on board. We had already stripped the hatches so the off-loading started without delay. N°3 and N°4 hatches contained part of a large consignment of Scotch Whisky and they were the first to be discharged under the watchful eye of plain-clothes Customs Officers. The Bosun, 'Chuck' Connor, was a tall, red-haired man in his forties and a keep-fit fanatic. He came from Stanley Road in the Kirkdale area of Liverpool. He put his head round the Mess Room door.

"OK, lads, all hands up to the Ship's Saloon. Usual thing, immigration interviews."

I'd been through all of this before and it was never very different. When it was my turn I stood in front of the seated Immigration Officer.

"Have you ever been deported from any part of the United States of America?"

"No, sir."

"Do you have any communist inclinations?"

"No. sir."

"Is there any insanity in your family?"

"No, sir." I heard a story off one ship of a sailor who, when asked this question answered "Yes, sir, my sister married a Yank!" He was arrested and put in prison for the duration of the ship's stay and fined $50 for insubordination. The Yanks don't mess about.

When Pongo was interviewed, he was asked to wait to one side and the Chief Officer was asked to attend when they brought him back. The Immigration Officer looked at Pongo.

"Is your full name Frank James Waring?"

"Yes, sir."

"Am I right in saying that on 6th May 1947 you were deported from Boston, Massachusets, back to the UK?"

"Yes, sir."

"Well, Mr Waring, I have to tell you, you will not be allowed to enter the USA. If you happen to go ashore here in New York, you will be arrested and taken to Ellis Island until your ship leaves and your Ship's Master will be fined."

The Immigration Officer then turned to the Chief Officer.

"This man is now your responsibility, sir."

The Chief Officer called Pongo over to one side.

"You know the score, Waring, don't let me down. There are lots of books on board and I'm sure the Chief Steward will be a little benevolent with a few extra beers when you finish work."

What didn't help matters was that night on his way ashore, one of the ABs shouted up to Pongo, "Never mind, Pongo! You've got plenty of time now to have that shower you haven't had since we left Liverpool!"

Pongo had had enough and slung a handful of plates after the AB. Most of the lads got back about midnight and some of them had brought a few bottles back for Pongo. There was plenty of room on the *Fort Musquaro*, so by popular demand Pongo had his own cabin. A couple of the lads, Monkey and Paul Byrne, knocked on his cabin door but got no reply.

"Poor sod!" said Monkey, "he's probably had an early night."

"Yeah," said Paul, "we're all boozing up in the Big Apple and poor old Pongo's tucked up in there with a good book."

Monkey knocked again, then quietly opened the door and there lying flat on his back was Pongo, in a drunken coma with a severely depleted crate of whisky by his side!

Chapter 11
Scotch Missed!

Pongo had somehow managed to get down into the hatch and helped himself to a case of Scotch Whisky. He'd emptied the contents of one bottle and was making in-roads on a second when he had passed out.

Paul shook his head. "If he gets caught with that lot he'll end up in bloody prison!" He took the remaining bottles out of the carton and got rid of the cardboard box. The rest of the Scotch was distributed amongst the sailors and firemen, which, short of pouring it down the sink, was just about the quickest way of removing the incriminating evidence.

Before long, the lads had discharged the hold of a good part of its liquid cargo, so if Pongo was in trouble now, he was in good company. By the time the Chief Officer and Customs Officers got onto it there must have been at least a dozen cases missing. As luck would have it, when they investigated further, there was a serious depletion in the Scotch cargo deep in the Lower Hold which none of the crew could possibly have got to.

"Looks like we lost it in Liverpool," the Chief Officer said. It was a stroke of luck. Everything that was missing was put down to the dockers or the shore gangs back home.

"You were lucky it was us who found you, Pongo!" Monkey said to him later, "and you were bloody lucky somebody had been at it before you!"

"Bloody bastards!" said Pongo, hardly remorseful, "serves 'em right!"

"What were you thinking of, anyway?" asked Paul, "you couldn't have thought you'd get away with it?"

"Couldn't care less," said Pongo, nursing a giant size hangover. He wasn't the best looking bloke in the world at the best of times. That morning he looked like death warmed up.

"Clears up one mystery, though," said Chuck Connor, the Bosun, who knew very well what had gone on, but had turned a blind eye. "Now we know why we had tractors running up and down the hold on the way out. The shore gang would have been too pissed to tie their boot laces, never mind lash down the cargo!"

"Must have been like New Year's Eve down there!" said Monkey, seeing the funny side.

"Yeah, no doubt!" said Chuck, who didn't. "But we haven't heard the last of this, I'm telling yer."

We left New York for Newport News with a part cargo. I'd never heard of the place but was told it was a large commercial city in Warwick County, Virginia, famous for its marine shipbuilding. They built all kinds of boats and ships, including Liberty Ships which were regarded as emergency vessels with only a five year life span but could be thrown together in a matter of weeks. I sailed on one once, though that was about fifteen years old, but they could only do about ten knots at full steam on a flat sea, and eventually they were scrapped.

We were in Newport one night when Big Paddy, Shoulders and Monkey got into a fight with some local lads. The favourite argument with the 'Yanks' and 'Limeys' was who actually won the war for the Allies.

"You were gettin' your goddamn arses kicked until Uncle Sam stepped in!" a US Marine argued.

"You took yer bleedin' time gettin' 'stepped in', didn't yer?" replied Monkey.

On this occasion our lads were seriously outnumbered, but that didn't stop Monkey, about 5-feet-5 and 9 stone, throwing the first punch. It had no effect. The Marine just looked at Monkey, picked him up and threw him across to the other side of the bar like a rag-doll. Big Paddy and Shoulders were holding their own and enjoying themselves when the Military Police arrived.

It took a dozen of them to do it, but eventually they managed to break up the fight and get handcuffs onto Paddy and Shoulders. They wrestled them out of the bar, threw them into the back of a jeep and took them to the 'jug' They had no problems with

Monkey. He'd started it, but certainly hadn't finished it. They dragged him off by the scruff of his neck and threw him into the next jeep.

Two days later they were escorted back to the ship looking a lot more subdued than the last time anyone saw them. They were a rather pathetic looking sight, covered in cuts and bruises, and looking as though they'd been in a real battle which, of course, they had. The next day the three of them were up in front of the old man. They were stopped two days pay and fined a further ten shillings for the two days they were 'adrift'.

The next day we left Newport News bound for Norfolk, Virginia, to collect a cargo of tobacco for Liverpool. We arrived a few days later on the Monday morning and started loading straight away. Norfolk, like Newport, was known as a quick turn-around port and we were only going to be there for three days. Longshoreman, as their dockers were called, were well paid and were worth their money. I spent most of my three days with the other younger lads at the Mission. We were well looked after and I can still remember that these places were a real Godsend for us younger fellas. Most of the staff there were voluntary, which made it all the more creditworthy. There were Snooker and Pool tables, TV and plenty of barn dancing if that's what you liked.

With the ship loaded, all hatches battened down, derricks lowered and secured and ready for sea the orders came from the Bridge. "Single-up to one head rope, Mr Mate!"

"Let go fore and aft!"

"Hold on to your Spring Rope!"

And then finally "Let go of your Spring!".

We were homeward bound for Liverpool.

★ ★ ★ ★

Three days out of Norfolk, I was on the twelve-four Watch on the Forecastle Look-Out. There was a lazy swell wind, S.W. Moderate. I was watching the thick black smoke billowing from the funnel and thinking about the poor trimmers below. At that time it would be young Frank McLean and his dad, turning to. Frank would be up and down the plank with his barrow full of coal trimming it to the fireman.

On Saturday the sailors and firemen brought out their ration of ale which they'd been saving at two cans a day and settled down to another performance of the Foo Foo Band. Despite his battlescars Monkey took to the floor to start proceedings. Poor old Monkey had taken one hiding off the sailors in the bar, another off the Military Police and, not to be left out, was turned over again by the Civil Police. If he lost a lot of blood he never lost his sense of humour.

Pongo shouted out, "Give us 'I Get a Kick out of You', Monkey! Ha! Ha! Ha!" Pongo thought his joke was hyterical.

"Oh, very funny Pongo!"

Paddy piped up, bruised and battered himself, "I remember one day in the Honky Tonk, this bloke goes over to 'Shoulders' and says 'Excuse me, mate, can you tell me the quickest way to get to Broadgreen Hospital?' And 'Shoulders' points to me and says, 'You see that big fella over there with the broken nose and the cauliflower ear?' And this fella says 'Yeah!' 'Well go and take a sip of his ale and I promise yer yer'll wake up in Broadgreen Hospital!'"

That went down well but the laughs turned to groans as Pongo started to get to his feet. Old Frank Whittaker saved the day by beating him to it. Much to everybody's surprise, instead of one of his famous poems. he launched into a melodic old sea-shanty ...

> "The heavy weather sails, boys
> That swept her round the Horn
> Are bleached with wind and rain, boys
> And some of them are torn.

> Tomorrow we'll unbend them
> And send them all below
> And up aloft my hearties
> Her tropic draperies go."

As soon as he'd finished, he was off again. With another shanty from his whaling days ...

> "It was seventeen-hundred and eighty four
> In March, the seventeenth day
> We weighed our anchor to our bow
> And for Greenland bore away, brave boys
> And for Greenland bore away.

> The Captain stood in the barrel aloft
> And the ice was in his eye
> Overhaul! Overhaul! Let your jib sheets fall!

And put your boats to sea, brave boys
And put your boats to sea."

The song told the story of a whaling ship hunting down its prey and the loss of over half-a-dozen sailors in heavy seas. He finally finished with ...

"Oh, the losing of those six jolly tars
It grieved our Captain sore
But the losing of that hundred barrel whale
Oh it grieved him ten times more, brave boys
It grieved him ten times more."

All hands were most impressed by this effort of Frank's and he was allowed another recital that finished like this ...

"And we laid him in a sailor's grave
Where the drooping willows grew
On a foreign strand
In a far-off land
On the golden coast, Peru."

Chuck, the Bosun, was next and with a can of beer in his hand said "Thank you very much, shipmates. I'd like to give the 'Sailing Ship Alphabet' and it goes like this ...

"A for the anchor which hangs from the bow
B for the bowsprit which weathers the blow.
C for the capstain we merrily man
D for the davits from which our boats hang.
E for the ensign which floats from our peak
F for the Fo'c'sle where sailors sleep.

G for the galley where coffee smells strong
H for the halliards we hoist to a song.
I for the iron which will some day rust
J for the jackstay to which we must trust.
K for the kulsun so far down below
L for the lanyards which stand a good blow.
M for the mast so tall and so stout
N for the needle which points the way out.
O for the oars which we bend with a will
P for the pinnacle which seldom will fill.
Q for the quarter where officers pace
R for the ratlins up which we all race.
S for the staysails so narrow but strong
T for the topsails which send us along.
U for the Union 'neath which we all sail
V for the vane which streams out to the gale.
W the wheel where we stand to our time
And the last three letters
Won't come into rhyme!"

We had a nice steady voyage homeward and managed to get a fair bit of painting done, quite a feat on the 'western ocean run'. We arrived back in Liverpool with our tobacco which would be taken to Stanley Warehouse up the road in Kirkdale, the largest of its kind in the world.

The next day we were paid off at Huskisson Dock and some of the lads dropped into 'Broken Nose Jacks' for a drink. Others went to the 'Corner of Sandhills', a pub actually called 'The

Sandhills' at the bottom corner of a road called Sandhills, but everybody called it the 'Corner of Sandhills'. Late in the afternoon, Monkey with the benefit of a few ales under his belt went back over the road to the ship. He made his way aft as if going to the accommodation, but in fact he headed for the Steering Flat. Hidden underneath the steering quadrant were ten plugs of tobacco and a dozen pairs of stockings, which Monkey stuffed down his shirt.

He walked back along the deck, had a chat with a couple of dockers and was about to make his way down the gangplank when he was approached by two men. They were both dressed as dockers, but they had obviously been watching Monkey. One of them blocked the gangway and said,

"Excuse me, sir, we are Customs Officers, and we believe that you have goods in your possession that should have been declared."

They produced their identity cards and escorted him to the ship's Saloon. There he was met by a 'Four Ringer', the Chief Customs Officer.

"We are confiscating these goods," he said. "You have a choice of going to court or paying a fine here and now. What do you wish?"

Monkey chose to pay the fine, fifteen pounds, and peeled of three crispy white fivers, three-quarters of his pay-off. It was the Bosun who had said we hadn't heard the last of the Scotch going missing, and he was right. From when the ship docked, the Customs Officers had been watching her like a hawk. They weren't looking for Monkey with his nylons and 'baccy', but he has walked into a trap laid for others. It was a hefty fine to pay and all for the love of a barmaid at 'Broken Nose Jacks'!

Chapter 12
Press Gangs

I did another couple of trips on the *Fort Musquarro* and left her in January 1949. She had a happy crew and I enjoyed my time with her, but I was young and I wanted to see more of the world.

After three weeks ashore, I signed up with another Cunard Boat, the *SS Bantria*. She was a small coal burner, one of four Mediterranean boats belonging to the company at the time, the others being the *SS Bactria*, the *SS Bothnia* and the *SS Bosnia*. They were all about 5,000 tons gross with a service speed of eleven-twelve knots. They were known to seamen as the 'Cunard Medi Boats'.

The *Bantria* left Liverpool on the 19th February and our first port of call was Gibraltar to off-load some cargo and take bunkers, coal and water. In Gibraltar I went ashore with the Deck-Boy, Johno, and after a brief visit to a bar, went for a walk around the Rock. We got talking to an old-timer who was eighty if he was a day. He told us the Rock rose fourteen hundred feet out of the

The Empire McDermott

The Derryheen

The Fort Musquarro, 1944

The Inventor, 1935

The Bantria

The Zungeru

The Debrett, 1940

The Cabano

The Britannic

The Beechmore, 1954

The Captain and crew of the Samaria, 1953

The Captain and crew of the Franconia, 1956

The San Cirilo, 1937

The Samaria, 1921

The Reina del Pacifico

The Parthia at New York, April 1948

*Tommy Miller, aged
21, as pictured in his
discharge book dated
July 1952*

*Working his way up
through the ranks*

*Tommy, retired now,
but with a wealth of
memories from his
seafaring days*

The Paraguay, 1944

The El Mirlo, 1930

The Arabia, 1947

The Scythia

The Florian, 1955

Tommy with two survivors of the Titanic

Mediterranean. The ancients had called it, together with its companion Gebel Musa on the African Coast, 'The Pillars of Hercules'. The Arabs were the first to recognise its strategic value, and when the Moors crossed the Straits in AD711 they christened it 'Gebel El Tarik' and built a castle there, the remains of which still overlook the Bay.

After a two day stop at 'Jib' our next ports were Izmir in Turkey and Thessaloniki in Greece. At the time we were one of the few ships to use the Corinth Canal, which separated Peloponnesia from the Greek mainland about thirty-five miles west of Athens.

One afternoon on Watch I was privvy to a discussion between the local Pilot and our Captian, a man called Bridgewater, about the history of the Canal. In very good English the Pilot explained.

"The Romans were the first to try and build a canal here across the four mile wide Isthmus of Corinth. It would have brought Piraeus, the port serving Athens, two hundred miles closer to the Adriatic, However, it was never more than an idea.

Captain Bridgewater was interested, but I was fascinated.

"It wasn't until about sixty odd years ago, in 1881, that a company was formed for the purpose of building a canal here and it was completed twelve years later. In terms of canal construction that is not a very long time but it is only four miles long and about seventy feet by twenty-six feet deep. Still, it is one of the wonders of the world, is it not?"

We stayed in Thessaloniki before crossing the Aegean Sea and spending another two days in Izmir. The next stop was Istanbul, which meant following the Turkish coast round to the north and passing the Dardanelles. Our Bosun, a little fella by the name of Turner, had been on this run for ten years and he told of the narrow strait which separates European Turkey from Asian Turkey and opens into the Sea of Marmara.

"That's the Gallipoli Peninsular!" he said, pointing over the port side. "You wouldn't think it now, it's so quiet, but in the First World War, on the 25th April 1915, the Allied Forces landed thousands of troops there, mostly Australians. They were bloody slaughtered, Tommy, bloody slaughtered."

I stared across quite solemnly and, indeed, it was difficult to imagine. Looking across at the mountains, the Bosun shook his head. "That was one battle we didn't bloody win, Tommy."

We arrived at Istanbul and tied up to the buoys in mid-stream. The Lighters, or barges, were brought alongside. We off-loaded our cargo and took on fruit for Liverpool. I took a small sub and with the other lads went ashore. We had a look round the city and took in a few bars. We had a fine time, apart form the Galley-Boy, a little worse for wear, wanting to scrap with one of the trimmers. It was all pretty pretty stuff. The Galley-Boy accused the trimmer of coming into the Mess with his hob-nail boots on and he in turn accused the Galley-Boy of not cutting the eyes out of spuds. Heavy stuff!

We got back about midnight and to everyone's surprise the Chief, Second and Third Officers were looking over the ship's side. There was a lot of activity but we were about to go into our accommodation when the Chief Officer called out.

"Stay where you are!"

Everybody stopped and looked around.

"I will tell you when you can go below."

We soon cottoned on to what was happening. Three ABs and two firemen were off-loading stolen cargo into one of the 'bum' boats, but unbeknown to them the Police had been tipped off and they too, were watching them. The cargo was loaded and the lads were being paid there and then in American dollars. The 'bum' boat was about to pull away when the Police boat arrived with its sharllights on full beam.

The 'bum' boat men and the seamen were arrested and taken away. The next day the ABs and firemen were returned to the ship under escort and shortly afterwards we set sail for Liverpool.

The five men were later brought up before the Captain. He didn't mince his words.

"You have committed one of the worst crimes in the book, that of sea-broaching cargo. This saddens me more than you know. You are all good seamen and I have sailed with each of you for some time now, but the Law of the Sea must be obeyed. When we return to the UK you will be given a 'Bad Discharge' for your conduct and it is possible you will be prosecuted by the Company."

A 'Bad Discharge' was known throughout the Merchant Service as a 'DR', which literally stood for Decline to Report.

As it happened, at Liverpool, although they each received their

'DRs', they weren't prosecuted but were dismissed from the employment of the Cunard Line 'sine die'. A 'DR' also meant it would be difficult for them to pick up any other ship, but in practice this lasted until Christmas. A week or so before Christmas it was very difficult for the Shipping Federation to crew a ship. As sailing days got nearer so some of these DR lads would be given a second chance.

One mate of mine, Bill Lee had a typical experience. He'd been told he could throw his Seaman's Book to the back of the fire because his seafaring days were over. He'd been given a 'DR' for punching an officer and even if we all felt tempted to do it on more than one occasion, there were few worse things you could do.

Anyway, a few months later he was about to sit down with his family to what they could muster together for Christmas dinner when there was a knock on the door. Bill opened the door and was confronted by one of the shipping clerks.

"Mr Lee?"

"Yes."

"We are desperately in need of a crew for a tanker bound for the Persian Gulf. With regard to your problems with the Shipping Federation we thought we would give you an opportunity to show your worth and give you another chance."

Bill had been unemployed since the Spring and was going through a very tough time. He didn't really have any choice.

"OK, when does she sail?"

"In about two hours, you'll have to come with me now in this taxi."

"Can you get an Advance Note to me missus?"

"Yes, that can be arranged."

So Bill went back inside, told his wife and with tears of both sadness and relief she waved Bill off, sitting in the back of the taxi finishing his Christmas dinner. The same thing was repeated at a few more houses.

"You know," Bill said to me years later, "it was just like a modern version of the old bloody Press Gangs!"

★ ★ ★ ★

I sailed with the *Bantria* on two or more occasions up to July 1949 although one trip was only a six day hop down to the South coast. I was home for ten clays and signed up with the *MV Beaverburn,* owned by the Canadian Pacific Steamship Company of Liverpool, a ship I had first set eyes on in Montreal on my very first trip, over two years ago. She was 8,000 tons with a surface speed of fourteen knots. Her yellow funnels with red and white panels were the same as the CPS Liners, but unlike their clean white hulls, her's was black. At the time, the CPS also owned the *MV Beaverford, MV Beaverlodge* and the *MV Beavercove* out of Liverpool and also the *MV Beaverbrey* who flew the Canadian flag and had a Canadian crew and officers.

Like the *Empire McDermott,* the *Beaverburn* ran to Montreal and over a period of four months to November I sailed with her four times. She was a happy ship, a good 'feeder' and there was plenty of overtime. She was known as a 'good money ship' by the lads who worked her, but I was looking for more than good wages and left her to join the *Esso London*, an oil tanker running to the Persian Gulf. She was a T2 Class with turbo-electric engines and by the standards of the day she was very modern. Originally, she had sailed under the American flag but had recently been bought by a British consortium.

Her accommodation had been up to the standard of a four-star hotel. Below decks she was fitted with an automatic washing machine, a fridge, ice-cold water fountains, a well-stocked library and a spacious recreating room. There were only two seamen to a cabin, each with their own wash basins, fitted wardrobes, writing desks and wooden desks. That was, of course, as an American ship. No sooner had she been bought than the leisure room was converted to a store room, the washing machine and fridge removed, the drinking-fountains ripped out and the cabins gutted and converted to four berths with steel bunks. Looking back it was quite disgraceful, but in those days it was nothing more than we were used to. During the war our servicemen were never as well paid or kitted out as the Americans and British ship owners thought more of the ship's cat than they did of the crew.

Chief Stewards weren't much better. Each crew member was allowed a certain minimum amount of basic foodstuffs, but in practice if it was stated as "5ozs of dried fruit", that was exactly what you got, meticulously weighed out. Most Chief Steward's were nicknamed 'belly robbers' and denied men their rations to make extra cash. A lot of stewards came from working class areas like Scotland Road or Kirkdale and were just ordinary lads. Those that made it to Chief Stewards, though, underwent personality changes and many of them moved out to better class areas such as Ainsdale and Hoylake. They would talk less and less about football but would wax lyrical about the latest improvement in their gold handicap.

One particular 'ruse' was to give the lads one egg for breakfast when they were entitled to two. It was accompanied with some fancy excuse but in truth meant they had half a dozen boxes to sell on to local traders at the end of the trip. I knew one who was particularly ruthless with the eggs and to this day, although he retired many years ago, is still known around Liverpool as 'One Egg Riley'!

★ ★ ★ ★

We were bound for Abadan near the Iraqi border of Iran at the northern most part of the Persian Gulf. I hadn't realised just how much monotonous work there was to do on a tanker. There seemed no end to the tanker-cleaning. One thing we had to look forward to each day was a large rum off the Chief Officer. If nothing else it cleared the nose for a few minutes from the constant smell of oil.

We took seventeen days to Abadan and it was tank-cleaning all the way. On arrival we took on crude oil straight away. When we were ready to go ashore one of the lads suggested a 'nice little bar' he knew. It was nice and it was little but only served goats milk and orange juice! Iran is a 'dry' country and it was only their suntans that spared the blushes of the hardened drinkers!

After a couple of days we were 'scupper' deep and Southampton bound. The Cook and Second Cook were both from Garston in the south end of Liverpool. If the Second Cook could be persuaded to take a shower every now and again, the Cook himself had obviously never been told where they were. Two ABs from Surrey, Bill and George, particularly objected to the lack of hygiene, but went a strange way about showing it.

The Cook wore size twelve hob-nail boots whenever he was working in the Galley and when he was done, he left them by the door. One night, Bill took the boots to the toilet and came back ten minutes later with one boot bearing the contents of his ablutions. The following day, with all hands expecting blue murder, the Cook went about his duties as if nothing had happened. He was either too embarrassed to make a scene or he was up to something.

On the menu that night was chicken curry and rice and, as usual, it was excellent. Bill and George took a couple of mouthfuls of their meal and were pretty quickly pulling faces.

"This curry tastes bleedin' awful!" said Bill.

The cook was quietly smirking. He'd obviously added his own ingredients to their meal. "Nobody else has complained, only you two shit-stirring bastards!"

Of course, he was right. Most of the lads got up for a second-helping, including me.

At Southampton we were paid off and most of the lads went to a well known pub near the docks called 'The Horse & Groom'.

We'd had a few beers when Bill went up to the cook.

"By the way, it was me who had a crap in your boots!"

"Yes, I know," the Cook replied, picking up his pint, "and it was you who ate it in your chicken curry and rice!"

Chapter 13
Tombo Mary's Bar

I was no lover of tank-cleaning and wasn't tempted to rejoin the *Esso London*. Eight days after docking at Southampton I signed up with the Eider Dempster & Co. of Liverpool and joined the *SS Zungeru*. She was 7,272 gross tons and had been one of the American Liberty ships I described earlier. They were mass produced, prefabricated vessels with welded hulls. Although they were generally regarded as being unsafe, they would normally outlive their life expectancy by ten years or more without any problems.

We left Liverpool on 31st January 1950 and headed first for Las Palmas in the Canary Islands, off the west coast Of Morocco. We off-loaded some cargo and took on fuel and although we'd hardly been away long enough to earn any wages the Chief Steward was reasonable enough to let us all have a 'sub'.

We made a tour of the bars and I got chatting to a local school teacher who told me about the Canary Isles. I'd been going away for nearly three years by this time but I was still only nineteen and keen to take all this in. The islands were mainly volcanic and were what remained of a peninsular reaching out from Morocco. They were first inhabited by the barbarians of Mauretania and were famous for a breed of dog, huge in size, from which one, Canavia, takes its name. He'd have told me a lot more but the lads were keen to move on so I bid him farewell.

We left Las Palmas and headed for Freetown in Sierra Leone. Years ago Sierra Leone was known as the 'White Man's Grave' owing to the number of diseases from which foreigners had no immunity. We picked up about forty native 'crew boys' to work the coastal ports. They were only paid 1s.6d a day, but there was nothing they wouldn't do. They worked from eight in the morning until midnight, chipping the decks, washing the crews clothes, painting, loading and off-loading and generally anything they were asked. They slept under the cargo hatch covers slung from the derricks like wigwams.

They weren't allowed below decks and the ship's 'chippy' had to knock together a toilet at the stern end of the ship. To use it they had to climb over the ship's rail and crouch over a small platform. They called it the 'African Ensign' and it certainly stopped the lads poking their heads out of the port-hole.

★ ★ ★ ★

Our next port of call was Abidjan on the Ivory Coast. It was there the 'crew boys' really got to work. In a sixteen hour day they stopped for an hour in mid-afternoon for a meal of yams and palm oil chops, which, incidentally, were delicious. Next stop was

Accra in Ghana in the Gulf of Guinea, formerly the capital of the Gold Coast, a British Colony.

We had to lie off the land because of the shallow water and before long the Lighters were towed out to us for off-loading. We were also joined by about twenty surf boats, thirty five feet long with a seven foot beam. Each was manned by a crew of four and would be loaded with cargo up to two tons. Two men for'd and two aft would then physically row the boats back to the quayside. If was an amazing sight and I'd challenge the strongest of our rowers to keep up with them. As they pulled away one of the men at the bow would start up a chant which the others would follow to the rhythm of their strokes. They were paid on the number of loads they brought in and this chanting kept their speed up.

From Accra we sailed through the Bight of Benin to Lagos, in the south-west corner of Nigeria near its border with Benin. There was always an old-timer on board who was happy to give me the details of any part of the world we were in. So I learned that Lagos was on an island joined to the mainland by a bridge. It had large floating docks and wharves and was connected by rail to Kano and Maiduguri over seven hundred miles to the north-east. This rail-line cuts right across the country linking up up a valuable export trade in palm oil, kernels, cotton, cocoa, ground nuts, hides and rubber.

We had to tie-up to buoys at Lagos as there were no land based docks and this was no easy task. The old man had earlier given the order to pull out the insurance wires which produced the general response of "Oh, bloody hell!" By international law all ships had to carry four inch insurance wires, the heaviest lines on board. They were used when mooring was particularly hazardous and they were the devil to work with. Tying-up generally took about an hour but this took at least four.

Next day we took on a cargo of logs, enormous things weighing as much as seven tons each. Everything was going well enough until the heavens opened and a gale blew up. A Panama ship tied up just ahead broke her mooring lines and had to put to sea. The old man's wisdom in using the insurance wires was now beyond argument.

We spent ten days in Lagos and hit most of the bars. We got into a game of football against the officers of the Railway Club, winning 4-0. We weren't invited back to the club, which might have been bad sportsmanship, but was more than likely good old-fashioned English Snobbery.

One of the crew boys headmen invited us all to join them on a night out and as we were all fond of them we were happy to accept. The crew boys were sacked if they were caught drinking when they were working so they hadn't been out for three weeks. The trip, though, was coming to an end, so they were ready to let their hair down.

As we were still moored someway off shore, the headman organised half-a-dozen canoes to ferry us ashore to Apper, just across the river. The crew boys wore their very best multi-coloured robes and we turned out in singlets and shorts. A right motley looking crew, to say the least.

We landed on the beach, about a dozen seamen and twice as many crew boys. "I will take you", boomed the headman, "first to Tombo Mary's Bar and then we go into the bush to the 'Jungle Bar!'"

Tombo Mary was an enormous woman, with eyes like saucers. Her skin was more copper than black and her teeth shone like white pearls. She was called after a local brew she served, which was pure dynamite. No wonder the locals could shin up a coconut tree like squirrels! The crew boys were dancing to the tom-toms and Mary herself knew how to move.

"You come and join me, nice boys!" she shouted over to us. One of the lads jumped up.

"If I'm not back in half an hour," he shouted over his shoulder, "send a bloody search party!"

"You must be jokin', Mac!" Tommy Wilson called back. "she'll suffocate yer in thirty bleedin' seconds!"

We were there for a couple of hours then finally the headman called out, "Right, my friends, now we go into the bush to the wonderful 'Jungle Bar'!"

Mary was not a happy woman. "You stay!" she wailed, "I make drink cheaper for you!" The headman waved her away and we stepped back out into the sunshine.

We walked about a mile through the bush, though some of the lads were feeling the effect of the Tombo and walked a lot further. Mary had been plying us with drink in the hope we would stay the night. After about twenty minutes we turned up at the Jungle Bar, which was in fact a large mud hut. There were no windows and inside there burned several paraffin lamps which shed some light on the hut and discouraged the mosquitoes. In one corner stood a huge fridge.

"Blimey!" said 'Jock' Murdoch, "a mud hut with all mod cons!"

As it happened, there was no electricity within a mile of the Jungle Bar, so it couldn't he 'plugged-in'. It had no works inside and was nothing more than a fancy cupboard. The beer was as warm as the room, but they seemed very proud of their fridge. I looked around and in one corner was a huge brass bed and in another a grand-piano. I walked over to the piano and could hardly believe it.

"Bloody hell, lads, look at this!"

On the piano-lid was the name, written in gold,

'Rushworth & Dreaper, Liverpool'

A couple of the lads walked over.

"How the hell did that find its way here?" said 'Slim' Nichols, an AB. Rushworth & Dreaper is still a thriving musical store in Whitechapel, Liverpool to this day, and I'm sure they would have been ingtrigued by an answer to Slim's question. Slim turned out to be a surprise package himself, as to ours and the locals delight, he lifted the lid and knocked out a few 'honky tonk' favourites. God knows how long it had been there, but the 'regulars' had never heard it played before.

The headman was in the company of two of his wives and

disappeared before long. It was a long and unusual evening. There we were in the African jungle, getting well-oiled, singing our favourite songs to an out of tune piano accompaniment.

We got back to the ship about five in the morning. and succeeded in waking everybody up, making our way back in the canoes, we were laughing and splashing about like young kids and it took the best part of an hour to negotiate the short distance to the ship.

We managed about three hours sleep before we had to turn-to, and coming on deck the Bosun gave me the job of painting the yardarm on the foremast. It was a job I could have done without, but the Bosun was getting his own back on all of us for breaking his sleep.

"Nesbitt, Broad, Murdoch, Jones − your job is over the side painting the stern. Collinson, Owens, Wilson − you're painting the main mast."

We hadn't yet sobered up and had to watch our step crawling all over the ship. As bad as we all felt, Davey Owens managed to get us laughing.

"Hey, Jock, I'd watch your head while you're painting the stern!"

"What d'yer mean?" said Jock.

"There's a hell of a bloody queue for the African Ensign this morning!"

Chapter 14
Bob the Bosun

Three months after leaving Liverpool we returned to fine weather and a clam sea at the end of April. The Liver Birds watched our progress up the river and looked as good as ever. Although I enjoyed coming home I was never back for more than a few days before I was itching to go again. After two weeks I signed up with the SS *Alca* bound for the Canary Islands. She belonged to Yearwards of Liverpool and was a small cruise liner, carrying about one hundred and seventy passengers and around 3,000 tons.

There was nothing but the best for the fare-paying passengers, but the accommodation and food for the crew was as it ever was. If she had one thing going for her it was her destinations, Lisbon, Madeira, Las Palmas, Sata Crux and Casablanca. She was generally a happy crew, but, like most, there was always one or two to spoil it. On this trip it was the Bosun, Bob and his mate the Lamptrimmer.

On most smaller ships the Lamptrimmer is the Bosun's assistant. Bob himself was about five-eight, well built and in his forties. His mate though was just the opposite, skinny but wiry with it. I was as fit as a fiddle and good at my job thanks to old Ted on the *Derryheen,* but neither of them took a shine to me. They tries any number of tricks to trip me up, but I always seemed to have an edge, which annoyed the Bosun all the more.

One of the worst jobs on board ship was bilge cleaning or bilge diving. This was cleaning the dirty oil and water from the bilges and the smell was absolutely dreadful. It gave Bob great pleasure having me do that and although I felt like throwing up I never let him know it.

When we got to Lisbon, I went ashore with the Deck-Boy and was enjoying a few pints in one bar when Bob and his mate walked in. They'd obviously had a fair bit to drink. He spotted me and swayed on his feet. He clenched his fists at his side before walking over to me.

"Do you think you know it all, do you?" he said, slightly slurring his words.

I knew what was on his mind, and it seemed to me as good a time as any to teach him a lesson. Before I could think anymore about it, he swung a punch at me but I was able to duck underneath it. Sitting next to me was a huge Norwegian about six-feet-six and sixteen stone if he was a pound. He took the blow solidly on the side of his chin. Standing up, he towered over Bob and gave him such a thump he flew over half-a-dozen tables. The Lamptrimmer decided to join in and he went the same way a few seconds later. We cleared the Canary Islands and sailed for Liverpool. Bob had his neck in a collar, the Lamptrimmer had his shoulder strapped up with his arm in a sling and I had a permanent smile on my face all the way home!

★ ★ ★ ★

In August I joined the *MV Potaro*, belonging to the Royal Mail Lines & Co. I now had three years sea-time experience and signed on as a Senior Ordinary Seaman, which meant a few extra quid. We left Liverpool bound for Dakar, West Africa, for refuelling and then made our way across the Atlantic for South America. The Atlantic was on her best behaviour and we had a steady passage to Recife in Brazil, over a thousand miles north of Rio de Janeiro.

We arrived on the day of the annual street carnival and when we'd finished work we went ashore and joined in. The festival had taken weeks to organise. Everywhere was awash with colour and all the women looked beautiful, even before we'd had anything to drink. After three days we left the 'Seaman's Paradise' of Recife and headed five hundred miles south to Salvador. We were there for a day off-loading a part cargo before moving on the the capital of the Brazilian states, Rio de Janeiro.

The entrance to the harbour offers a view of stunning beauty. Watching from the deck, the Sugarloaf Mountain comes into view and the Statue of Christ the Redeemer at the summit of the Coroowado Mountain overlooking the sea and country around the city. The statue is 1,200 feet high and the arms span ninety nine feet.

We were in Rio for a week and for a change all hands were as good as gold. There were no fighters aboard but the lads were always ready to have a laugh. We called at Porto Alegre and then on to Motevideo. At Motevideo I've never seen so many bars in one street! Nobody did much sightseeing but we got to know that street pretty well.

We then moved on to Buenos Aires, capital city and major seaport of Argentina. We spent ten days loading at Buenos Aires, a beautiful city. One difference I notices from the other ports of call was the mood of the people. In Brazil the locals were happy and friendly but here there was a lot of tension. There was a general animosity towards the British and this was a long time before the Falklands War. If you gave a sideways glance at one of the police officers you'd be banged up in the Calaboose or sweeping the streets. I'm not exaggerating. I was on the main street, Viente-Cinco de Mayo, when I saw this fella sweeping the street and I couldn't believe it when I recognised him – the Flying Flea! He'd been arrested for being drunk and was locked up each night after cleaning the streets for ten hours from seven o'clock in the morning. He would be there until the ship sailed.

"Just my bloody luck!" he snarled. "The ship's been stuck in this piss-hole for four weeks and I've been propping this bleedin' brush up for three of them."

There were few things so humiliating to see than a Brit sweeping the streets of Buenos Aires.

One outpost of the place was 'May Sullivan's Bar.' May was Irish but had lived in Buenos Aires since she was a girl. There was no trouble in there. Occasionally, some of the locals would try to stir something up, knowing the police would be on their side, but May knew how to handle them.

The Mission was another place of sanity and professionally run. Only for those two places it wouldn't have been worth going ashore. I enjoyed the boxing and football organised between the crews of the ships in port.

As with the Flying Flea's ship, some were in port at Buenos Aires for several weeks. Lads from the Blue Star, Lamport & Holt and the Royal Mail ships, all regular South American runs, would all compete for boxing and football trophies. At the time, Blue Star ships won most of the boxing trophies and Lamport & Holt the football trophies. Darts were also popular.

The Padres at the Mission were often pretty good boxers and all-round sportsmen. They would also sometimes act as councillors for seamen if they had a particular problem. They did an admirable job with a good attitude. While away at sea, a man could be faced with an agonising dilemma he could do nothing about for several weeks. Over the years I came across many men who received 'Dear John' letters from home when they were thousands of miles away. To some it came as a blessed relief, but the Padres were a great relief to those who took it badly.

We finally left Buenos Aires and I wasn't sorry to see the back of it. I didn't care if I never saw the place again.

★ ★ ★ ★

On the 20th November I signed on and sailed with the *MV*

Debrett of Lamport & Holts. It was my first trip as an AB and I was on a monthly wage of £22 for a fifty-six hour week. Once again I was bound for South America, but just before we sailed, one of the deck-hands had to leave the ship with 'domestic' problems and the Federation had to supply a stand-by for each of the ship's departments and when the replacement turned up I had a chuckle when I saw who it was. Bob, the Bosun who had thrown a punch at me in Lisbon made his way up the gangway, but this time coming aboard as an AB like myself.

He was no problem on board because nobody could get more than their beer ration. It was in port I'd have to watch him. He was wearing a beautiful Omega watch he'd bought for himself after a big pay-off. The watch had cost him £150 which in those days was a fortune. You're talking over six months pay for an AB.

We called at Recife, the Seaman's Paradise and most of the ports I'd done on the *Potaro*. Thankfully we weren't long at Buenos Aires and we went to one port I hadn't been to before, Bahia Blanca, the last port before returning home.

We were in a bar there and I noticed Bob, the ex-Bosun, drinking on his own. An American was sitting close by admiring his watch. He called across to Bob, "Hey, Limey! That's a nice watch you have there. Mind if I take a look at it?"

Bob didn't take it off his wrist, but he let the Yank have a good look at it.

"If you're thinking of selling it, buddy, I'll give you two hundred bucks."

Bob tossed this around in his head for a second, then shook his head.

"No, mate, nothing doing."

A couple of hours later Bob was on his way out and called to the Yank. "Give me three hundred bucks and the watch is yours."

The Yank studied the ceiling for a moment then smiled. "OK, Limey, it's a deal!" He counted out the money while Bob took off his watch and placed it on the table.

"You see that photograph on the wall over there, Limey?"

Bob looked to see a picture of a beautiful, semi-clad woman. "What about it?"

"I used to have a thing going with that lady."

Bob wasn't impressed. "Oh, really!"

"Sure did!" He gave Bob the money, picked up the watch and left. "See you, Limey."

Bob turned to the other lads who had been watching all this going on. "I'm going to have a ball with this!" He said, clutching the roll of notes. he called over to the barman. "Give the lads a drink!" He pealed a $50 note from the roll and his eyes nearly popped out of his head. All the other notes were made of pesoes, korunas, francs, rupees, yen and currencies nobody had ever heard of. The top bill was a genuine $50 note, he would have done well to pay a round of drinks with the rest. When the Yank had distracted Bob with the photograph, he had switched the rolls.

One of the lads, Sam McClusky, thought it was quite funny and started to chuckle quietly. Bob glared at him and picked up a bottle from the bar. I thought he was going to hit Sam with it but instead he threw it across the bar smashing a dozen or more bottles of spirits on the shelf. We had to get off pretty sharpish or we'd have all been locked up, and were just disappearing around the corner when the police arrived. In that part of the world the police take a delight in beating up British seamen and if you fight back it's been known for some lads to get shot.

Bob himself never got out and was locked up for a few days. There was no love lost between the pair of us but I felt sorry for him when he came back to the ship. He'd been beaten so badly he had to be helped up the gangway. He was his own worst enemy but he'd been conned out of his watch, the police had stolen what money he had left and he had been really knocked about.

We cleared the South American coast bound for London with a cargo of meat. We stopped off at Las Palmas for fuel and were delayed an extra day with engine problems. We were allowed ashore but weren't granted any subs. On a good ship lads would share out their money and that's what happened here.

The drink, thankfully, was very cheap and around midnight we decided to call it a day, all the worse for wear. I was just finishing my drink off when suddenly an arm was thrown around my neck, choking me so hard I couldn't breathe. It was Bob. If it hadn't been for the other lads who tore him away, he would certainly have killed me. He was in a drunken rage.

When I got back to the ship we locked the cabin door in case he fancied another go. When he was drunk you never knew what he was going to do and he was pretty sore with the world this time. I didn't sleep well that night and the following day I was late going in for breakfast. I sat down and Bob was there having a smoke, his empty breakfast plate pushed to one side. He looked at me with a smirk on his face.

"It seems I was out of order last night," he said.

I said nothing and got on with eating my breakfast. My mind though, was racing. I knew the rules. I knew that if I didn't sort this out it would happen again. My stomach churned because this was no easy thing to do. He was a very strong man.

On the drainboard was a large mug. I filled it with water and walked over to Bob, who was still sitting there having a smoke. I poured the contents of the mug over his head and he jumped up like a discharged cannon shot. He was throwing punches all over the place, but I was younger and fitter and able to duck under them. Even so, for a moment I thought he would overwhelm me until he started to blow for tugs and was struggling for breath. I managed to get a couple of hefty digs as my confidence grew, until finally he put up his hands to say he'd had enough. I was reluctant to accept this knowing that, although I'd won, I'd have to watch him like a hawk. In the end though, I let him go.

After that, he never bothered me again, although I never took my eyes off him when he was about. We docked at London and were paid off, and without any diversions, I made my way to Euston Station and Liverpool.

Chapter 15
Cook Adrift

A good friend, Johnny Molyneux, was getting married on February 24th so I made my mind up to look for another short trip. I'd heard from one of the lads that a small coaster, the *Denbigh Coast* was in port and an AB short. She was about 800 tons and took a crew of eight men. On going down to her, I made my way up the gangway to be met by the Chief Officer.

"Mornin', boyo!" he said. He was a bloody great beast of a man straight from the Welsh valleys. He was wearing a cloth cap and a black jersey covered in soup stains that looked a month old. It wasn't long before I understood the crew's fondness of soup.

I told him why I was there and handed him my seaman's book.

"I see you've been around then, boyo!" he said.

"Just a bit." I answered.

"There's lovely, then!" He returned my book. "She sails at half-ten tomorrow morning. Don't be late or we'll go without you."

"I'll be here."

The next day I met my shipmates and if there was one less than sixty years old I couldn't find him! They were a right bunch of old sea-dogs and no mistake. Each had sailed the world around and then some and were now settled into a nice little run that brought them home more weeks than it didn't.

I met the Captain, who was rigged out like his Chief Officer in cloth cap, black jersey and matching soup stains. He looked at my seaman's book but wasn't impressed.

"You'll be in for a rough ride!" he said.

"What do you mean by that?" I asked.

"This type of boat has a completely different motion to the big buggers you're used to!"

"I think I can handle it." I'd been going away for four years by this time and I felt I deserved more respect.

"Well, we'll find out soon enough, the wind's blowing in up the Bay." He turned to walk away but our attention was drawn to what resembled a tramp climbing the gangway. "Ah, there you are, then! This is the cook, he'll be after you for some money for the stores."

I took one look at the cook and thought if he came aboard some of the ships I'd been on he'd have been tossed straight over the side.

"You wouldn't happen to have a brother on the *Esso London*, would you?" I asked him.

"What are you talkin' about?" he grunted back.

"Never mind."

He wore a macintosh that had once been white but was now thick with grease. "Who are you, anyway?" he asked.

"I'm the new AB."

"Well, you have to give me seven-and-six for the stores." he said, holding out his hand.

"I don't have to give you anything! I can look after my own stores!"

"You won't be allowed in the galley!"

"Look at the state of you! I'd rather starve than have you cook for me!"

It was starting to get out of hand and the Captain stepped in.

"I'm afraid he's right," he said. "the galley's too small, you see. There's only one man allowed in there and that's him. You don't have a choice. You pay him or you don't eat."

I parted with 7s.6d. but I was less than happy about it.

We left Liverpool with a few tons of general cargo bound for Cardiff. After a few hours we ran into a Force Eight gale and it gave me no satisfaction to find the old man was right. I'd thought my days of being sea-sick were well behind me, but unlike the bigger ships that had a steady, lazy roll, the *Denbigh Coast* sailed through the water like a cork-screw. I had a bad time made worse watching the cook wipe his nose on his grease-covered sleeve.

We finally got into port a couple of days late and I was glad to get ashore for a few hours. We were supposed to spend a couple of days in dock turning the cargo round and were now due back in Liverpool on the friday, the day before the wedding. As it turned out the weather got no better and by Friday morning we were still weather-bound in Cardiff.

To make things worse, the cook had gone ashore on Wednesday and hadn't been seen since. At any other time this would have been cause for celebration, but he'd taken the Mess money with him and there was very little left to eat except soup. Nobody had any money to speak of and although I'd noticed this crew drank more soup than most, it was hardly a satisfactory state of affairs. Barney, the only other Scouser on board, sat at the Mess table staring at his fifth bowl of soup in two days.

"If my missus mentions bloody soup for dinner when I get home, I'll hit her with the bloody tin!"

By mid-afternoon I'd had enough and went to see the Captain. "I'm sorry, sir, but I can't stay with the ship any longer. I have to be in Liverpool tomorrow for a friend's wedding and I only took the trip because I thought I'd be home two days ago."

"It's a long walk home, boyo!"

"I thought I'd jump a train, sir, if you could sort my money out."

"No problem there, boyo, but you might have some trouble with the train. There's only one train each day to Liverpool and I'll be surprised if you haven't already missed it."

"I'd still like to try."

"As you wish. Come back in an hour and I'll have your money. If you have no luck come back to the ship. We're sailing at midnight and I'm not going to be able to replace you at this time on a Friday."

I thanked him and an hour later was in a cab heading for Cardiff Central.

When I got to the ticket-office I was greeted by a smiling clerk in his thirties. "Yes, sir?"

"Am I in time for the Liverpool train?"

"Oh, yes, plenty of time, sir! The train to Liverpool Lime Street doesn't depart until half-past-one tomorrow afternoon!"

"Oh! Bloody hell! What time does that get in?"

"Let me see, sir. That arrives at Liverpool at ... 19.42, that's nearly a quarter-to-seven, sir."

"Thanks." I walked away. There was no point in coming back the next day, I'd have missed the wedding and everybody would have been well-oiled by the time I got there.

On the bright side, I didn't have to go dashing back to the ship. I had some moeny so I could go for a few pints and a decent meal. After something to eat I walked around the city centre, taking in the pubs I fancied, slowly making my way towards the docks. I was walking down Bute Street and came across a pub called The Custom House, a couple of minutes walk from the ship. I walked in and the first thing I saw, sprawled on a table unconscious, was the cook! The barman looked up at me.

"Do you know him, then?" he asked.

"Yeah, we've been looking for him since Wednesday. I know it's hard to believe, but he's the ship's cook!"

"Yeah, well, when you go, take him with you, will you? He's been a bloody nuisance!"

I started to wake him up but as he came round he flew into a violent rage and started smashing furniture and throwing the pieces around the bar.

"Oh, right! That's it then!" said the barman, who picked up the phone and called the police. The police arrived within a couple of minutes and dragged him outside. I tried to calm him down and reason with the officers, but I was wasting my time. They threw him in the back of the patrol car and drove off. I walked back into the pub where the dust as beginning to settle.

"When do you sail?"

"Midnight."

"You'll be going hungry, then."

"I'll say! The police have got the cook and you've got the Mess money!"

The weather didn't improve much on the wy back to Liverpool and I thought I'd never get home. By the time we finally docked I was near starved to death and totally fed up. I made my way down the gangway and the Chief Officer called after me. "Are you coming back with us, boyo?"

"Only if everyone else sinks!" I called back.

Chapter 16
Three Wheels on my Wagon

I stayed with the Elder Dempster line for a while going back to the the west coast of Africa with the *S.S. Cabano* and the *M.V. Mary Kingsley*, named after the famous explorer. I was aboard the *Kingsley* over Christmas and New Year of 1952 and a week after I got home I signed up with the *S.S. Assyria* — a Cunard Line cargo boat.

She ran between Liverpool and Montreal or New York on regular trips. Every fourth Wednesday she would arrive in Liverpool and spend ten days off-loading and loading before making her way hack across the Atlantic. It was an ideal run if you were a married man, and there were many who stayed with this kind of ship for several years.

Over a period of ten months I made seven trips with the *Assyria*. She had a settled and happy crew, from the old man down who, incidentally, was an awesome darts player. If you could beat him you got yourself a double rum, but it didn't happen very often. He would call everybody by their first name, even the Galley-Boy. I remember the cook, 'Nogger' Willis, who had so many lines on his forehead we used to say he could have screwed his hat on.

In those days, you could buy a washing machine at the Salvation Army store on 42nd Street in New York for $5 which were practically brand new and a few of the lads had bought them. The only problem was when you got them back to Liverpool they had to he converted to the correct ampage which was different from the US and this cost about £7. However, because they were second-hand there was no customs duty so it still worked our cheaper than buying one at home. Most Captains would turn a blind eye when you hauled them on hoard, but if they wanted to be funny, or disliked, they were entitled to charge freight carriage.

On one trip, an Engineer had paid a deposit on a machine and as he was on watch he asked me if I'd pick it up for him.

"I don't mind" I said, "but how the hell am I going to get a washing machine from 42nd Street to here?"

"No problem," he replied, "I organised with the boss stevedore for someone to borrow a four-wheel truck."

I had no problem picking up the truck, but when I got to the store I could see I was going to have big problems picking up the washing machine. I took one look at it and nearly fell over when I saw the size of it. It would take four fit men to raise it a foot off the floor.

Outside the store there were about six or seven down-and-outs who were getting near the bottom of their last bottle of wine. I approached them and they were only too pleased to help if I could help them with a few bob. The mention of two dollars did the trick and with a rope secured to the back of the truck we somehow managed to get it on board. I set off and took a detour as I didn't fancy the truck's chances of getting up one particularly steep hill. I got onto the main road which ran into the Broadway area and before I knew it I was in the middle of New York's heaving commuter traffic. I'd never seen so many vehicles in my life. There was all kinds of horns blowing and people yelling.

"Goddammit! Get that truck out of the way."

"Hey! You son of a bitch, are you goddamm blind?"

It was in the middle of all this that the one of the rear wheels fell off and as the truck tilted and crashed to the ground the washing machine slid down the boards and crashed into the street. All hell broke loose and I thought I was going to be lynched. A Rolls Royce cruised past and a bloke sitting in the back smoking a huge cigar smiled at me as if he thought it was all quite amusing. It stopped me in my tracks, because I recognised him instantly as Frank Sinatra. Nobody ever believed me, but if it wasn't Ol' Blue Eyes it was his spitting image.

A big New York Irish cop strolled over and as soon as he saw me he knew I was English.

"What's the goddamm trouble here, Limey?"

With his help I managed to get the truck parked down a side

street and made myway back to the ship. I went straight to the Engineer who was happy to see me.

"There you are, Dusty! I thought you'd got lost!"

I blew my top.

"Lost! Bloody lost! You get me a cardboard box on three wheels and you ..."

"Three wheels?"

"It's got three bloody wheels now, hasn't it! One fell off in the middle of bloody Broadway!"

As I ranted I could see he was doing his level best not to laugh and I started to see the funny side of it myself. Within a few seconds we were both rolling around in stitches and as I tried to spit the story out we got worse. By the time I got to the part about Frank Sinatra we were nearly choking.

He made arrangements for the washing machine to be picked up and promised me a crate of beer for my trouble. For the rest of the trip every time he passed me, he burst into song ...

"Three wheels on my wagon
And I'm still rolling along
The cherokees are after..."

★ ★ ★ ★

Homeward bound the temperature dropped below freezing point. On the third night out of New York the Mast-Head Light went out and as one of the most important lights on the ship it had to be replaced immediately. Without it, the ship would be invisible and a quicker vessel could run into us before we got out of the way.

Technically, it was the electrician's job to change bulbs but more often than not one of the lad's would 'run up' the mast in return for a couple of cans of beer. I was on look-out and Tony Brady was at the wheel, so it fell to Chris Walker on stand-by to go up. Chris was a hard man who had spent most of his sea days on whaling ships and was, it seemed, immune to the cold.

Chris went aloft and after about ten minutes I began to wonder what was keeping him. I was on the Monkey Island and I could see him clearly enough, but he wasn't moving. I thought he must be having problems, so I lifted the voice box and called down to the Third Mate, Jack.

"I think Chris is having a bit of trouble up there."

Jack turned on the Eldis Lamp, with its powerful beam, onto the Mast-Head. Chris had his arms wrapped around the mast but he was absolutely still. Jack came back on the voice box.

"Dusty! Leave the look-out and get yourself up there. See what the problem is."

I was wearing a decent pair of gloves and pretty quickly got up to him. His face was screwed up in agony.

"What the hell's the matter?" I shouted.

"My hands!" he cried back.

The palms of his hands were frozen to the steel mast. It was difficult to get to him properly and each time I tried to pull him free he screamed with the pain. He was getting very distressed and it became a matter of urgency that I got him down as quick as I could. I took hold of his wrist and pulled for all I was worth. His hand came free, but most of his skin stayed where it was. Poor Chris nearly passed out with the pain. I got his other hand free the same way and slowly I managed to get him down.

When I got back on the deck I was completely exhausted, but my problems weren't worth talking about compared to Chris's. We did what we could to help him. His hands were heavily bandaged and the Chief Steward made sure he got plenty of rum to help him sleep.

I came across Chris some years later, but he wasn't the same hard man I'd known. The terror of what he'd been through had broken him. It was sad to see.

★ ★ ★ ★

On 19th October, always a glutton for punishment, I joined another tanker, the *S.S. San Cirilo*, belonging to the Eagle Oil Company. We sailed from Ellesmere Port bound once again for Abdan and within a couple of days I was bloody tank cleaning again!

There was so much gas in the tanks we could only stay down there for about five minutes at a time, though if the Chief Officer or the Bosun had had their way we'd have been down there a lot longer.

We had a powerful steam hose which took two men to hold. We blasted the water against the bulkheads for a few minutes and then we'd tug three times on the line leading up top. The lads on deck would then turn off the pressure and we'd come out.

The Chief and the Bosun were both huge blokes from Guernsey, and for reasons they kept to themselves they had no time for Liverpudlians. Mick O'Shaugnessy was only down the hatch for a few minutes before he could feel the effects of the gas and when he came up the Bosun had a go at him.

"You're just a malingering lazy bastard!" he said, at which Mick punched him square on the chin, nearly putting him over the side of the ship. The Chief thought about joining in, but decided against it and picked up the Bosun instead.

The next day, Mick and myself had to appear before the Captain with Mick on a disciplinary charge and me a witness. Both the Chief Officer and the Bosun were there and the Captain listened to all four versions of the event, which apart from the odd colourful detail, were more or less the same.

When we were all done, the Captain turned to the Bosun and, much to our surprise, said,

"You were totally out of order! If this man had been drunk when he hit you, well, that would have been a different matter. As it was, the man was full of gas and I am here to run a safe ship. I would also like to run a happy ship, so I would appreciate it if you both shook hands and apologised to each other."

The Bosun was the most reluctant of the two to do this, but the Captain insisted and afterwards the whole thing was more or less forgotten.

The ship was leaking oil like a sieve which wasn't as rare as ship owners liked to make out. We were having a lot of mechanical problems, but little did I know at the time that there would later be fatal consequences. All told, she broke down thirty five times before she limped into Newcastle on Christmas Day. Most of the lads thought she was more trouble than she was worth, but it hadn't been such a bad trip for me. I thought I might some day sail with the *San Cirilo* again some day, but instead a tragic end awaited her.

Chapter 17
The Run-Jobs

I signed on next with the *M.V. British Supremacy*, a tanker on a 'run-job' from Ellesmere Port to Falmouth in Cornwall. A 'run-job' is a single, short trip from one specified port to another, though the owners could divert you to others at their discretion. Seamen were paid by the mileage as follows:

Up to 50 Miles	@	5d per mile
51 to 100 Miles	@	4d per mile
101 to 150 Miles	@	3d per mile
151 to 300 Miles	@	2d per mile
301 to 500 Miles	@	1d per mile
501 plus Miles	@	½d per mile
Minimum payment		£1 2s 6d
Maximum payment		£6 0s 0d
Ordinary seamen and boys		Half Mileage rates

I was only with the *British Supremacy* for twelve days and a week later went to another 'run-job' to Hull on the *S.S. City of*

Cardiff, which took three weeks.

★ ★ ★ ★

At the end of February, 1953 I joined the Cunard Passenger Liner *S.S. Samaria* as Quartermaster. The job of the Q.M. was strictly steering the ship and hoisting or lowering the ship's flags as necessary. In port the Q.M. would keep an eye on the gangways.

I was proud of myself, aged twenty-one, steering, 19,848 tons of ship up the Hudson River and docking her at Pier 92. The American pilots had their own expressions, using right and left instead of starboard and port. The biggest difference between them and our own pilots was manners. The Americans would always say "Thank you, Quartermaster," before they left. You were lucky if an English pilot gave you the time of day.

The Q.M. was classed as a Petty Officer and was much respected by the Officers generally. There were six of us on board, each taking it in turn doing our 'trick' on the wheel.

Each ship has a 'Pig & Whistle' for the crew, where you can relax after coming off watch with a few beers. Unlike the cargo ships, the food on the passenger lines was excellent. Everybody ate well. In the 'Pig' there was usually something going on and the *Samaria* was no exception – a darts match, a game of cards or someone playing a piano or accordion.

One lad, who I had sailed with before, was the 'plate man', continually washing hundreds and hundreds of plates of crockery. One night we were having a drink, when he got up saying, "I won't be long," and ten minutes later he was back.

"You weren't long," I said, "where've you been?"

"I've been doing the dishes. I gave them a 'Yankee' wash."

"A 'Yankee' wash? What's that, then?"

"Well, we wash some of the plates and we chuck the rest out of the porthole. We'd be there all night otherwise."

"Do you do that much?"

"Every liner, every day, all the time," he smiled, "they reckon if the Atlantic Ocean ever dries up you'll be able to walk from Liverpool to New York just by following the plates!"

★ ★ ★ ★

The *Reina Del Pacifico* is a beautiful luxury liner, but amongst seamen she had a bad reputation. There was frequently trouble amongst the crew and she was for ever suffering from mechanical breakdowns. I joined her on 8th January 1954 as Quartermaster and the general opinion of my mates was I deserved a medal.

As far as I ws concerned, I was young, fit and I could handle myself if I had to. I wanted to see as much of the world as I could and the *Reina* gave me another opportunity. Before I signed-on I made my way down to the Canada Dock. There she loomed over the quay, her derricks swinging back and forth, her cargo nets full of goods bound for South America. As I looked up from the quayside she didn't look very glamorous. She had two dirty, buff-coloured, squat funnels. Her sides were a dull silver grey and her green boot-topping was crying out for a lick of paint. I'd seen better-looking trampships.

On board, although the passengers' accommodation was luxury

indeed, the facilities for the crew were depressing. It was almost as if the shipbuilders had thrown it together as an afterthought. For the Quartermasters it wasn't as bad. We were six to a cabin as opposed to eight or twelve.

Usually when coming aboard you would report to the Chief Officer, but on the *Reina* it was the Bosun. I found his cabin and through the open door I could see him sitting down puffing on his pipe. I knocked and he turned to reveal a colossal figure, who I got to know as 'La' Murphy, an Irishman. I never got to the bottom of his nickname, but it was probably due to him sailing out of Liverpool for donkey's years and 'la' is a Scouse expression for 'lad'.

I gave him my Seaman's Book and he flicked through its pages, taking his time.

"The job's yours, if you want it." He said.

"I do." I replied.

"She sails at noon on Thursday, you can sign on at ten-thirty in the morning."

My younger brother, Tony, had done three trips in her as the Plumber's Mate. I wasn't mad about the idea of sailing with him. If there was any trouble Tony would run a mile, whereas I was happy to be in the middle of it!

On the Thursday, we left the Canada Dock and headed for the Princess Landing Stage to pick up the passengers. I was on the twelve-four Watch with 'Bocker' Rawley. Usually, the 'Boss' Quartermaster takes the ship in and out of port, but on this occasion the 'Boss' was suffering from the effects of too many 'Aussie' white wines the night before in Yates' Wine Lodge and couldn't steer a cart. 'Bocker' wasn't much fitter, so the Bosun told me to take her out.

I went with Bocker up to the Bridge and we took our stations. I took the wheel and Bocker stood by on the wing of the Bridge. On the starboard wing stood Captain John Whitehouse, a surly, unapproachable man. His Staff Captain was a man called Allenby, just as cheerful and no easier to get on with.

An hour later we arrived at the Landing Stage and the gangway was secured. As a Quartermaster one of my duties was to man the gangway as the passengers came aboard. Next to me stood a steward who had been with the *Reina* for a few years and he provided me with a descriptive running commentary about each person who passed by.

"You see this bloke coming now?" He nudged me and indicated a smart, distinguished-looking gentleman in his fifties, "he's one of the best paying bloods that I know."

"Bloods?" I asked, "what's a blood?"

"Well," he began to explain. "We squeeze the passengers for as much as we can get out of them. With some of them it's like squeezing blood from a stone, but not him."

"Really." I replied. I wasn't impressed.

"I've known some bloods," he went on, "the really tight ones, who've had Goddards plate powder put in their soup. Gives them the 'wild trots' for a few days!"

"So if a fare paying passenger doesn't tip you properly, he ends up spending his trip on the pan."

"Serves them right!"

I took an instant dislike to this man. I was no soft touch for anybody, but I gave respect where I felt it was due and this was nothing but callous. As it happened, I had the last laugh on this particular specimen of low-life.

★ ★ ★ ★

We left Liverpool bound first for La Rochelle in France to pick up the French 'bloods'. There was no shore-leave there, but as we'd only been sailing for five minutes and most of the lads had brought their own booze aboard, nobody was very bothered. There was plenty of Australian white wine in the crew's lockers and by the time we'd arrived at La Rochelle there had already been half-a-dozen fights. Dancing with another man's girlfriend at the Grafton Rooms or the Orrell Park Ballroom seemed to be one of the main reasons.

As the French passengers came aboard the same steward made for a 'blood' he knew to be a good tipper.

"Good afternoon, I hope you have a good trip, Madam!" he said, gushing all over her. She looked at him like he was a piece of dirt.

"Excuse me," she answered in perfect English, but with a heavy French accent, "a madam is a brothel-keeper, are you suggesting I own a brothel?"

He went completely beetroot in colour. "Er...no, of course not!

I was just ..."

"Then you should address me as 'Madame' not 'Madam', though I would prefer it if you did not address me at all. Please get out of my way!"

I thought his chin was going to hit the floor as he stumbled backwards. One of his best-paying 'bloods' had just blown him out of the water. I enjoyed telling the rest of the lads about it, and for the rest of the trip, whenever he was in earshot, it was 'Madam this' and 'Madam that'.

We sailed form La Rochelle bound for Santanner in Spain and a few other small ports where we picked up the last of the passengers. I got to know most of the stewards on the way out and found them generally very professional. The Engine Room itself was filthy, with oil seeping all over the place and the temperature was usually in the hundreds. The hand-rails got so hot you had to wear gloves.

What really used to get the lads' backs up was the attitude of the Junior Engineers. When they came up for some fresh air they would see them playing deck games with the passengers in their starched white uniforms. They might have only been at sea for a few weeks, but they looked down on the ship's firemen and frequently complained at their presence. I overheard one fireman, a Liverpool lad, quietly threatening one of them.

"There's nothing I can do here, but don't let me catch you ashore!"

The Engine-Room was not a pleasant place to be.

I was chatting with one of the old-timers one morning a couple of days into the trip.

"Did you know that Ramsey MacDonald died on board this ship in 1937?"

One of the lads looked at him quite seriously. "Didn't he used to live in Scotty Road?"

"No, you daft bat! He was Britain's first Labour Prime Minister! The ship was going to South America and he took bad. He died in his cabin. The daughter, Sheila I think her name was, was with him when he went."

He went on to tell us about the *Reina* in September 1947. She had been re-fitted and was undergoing trials off Belfast Lough. There was a loud explosion and the Captain, John Whitehouse, thought the ship had hit a stray mine left over from the war. He made his way down to the Engine Room which was pitch black and thick with smoke. There were dead and injured men everywhere. In all, twenty-eight men were killed and another twenty-three injured. A piston had overheated and blown up. It was a terrible tragedy.

Chapter 18
Slip Sliding Away

Most of the ports we called at were, for the passengers anyway, 'day-excursion' stops. We visited Port of Spain in Trinidad and Bridgetown, Barbados, before sailing along the Venezualan coast to Caracas. From there we headed north-west across the Caribbean Sea to Kingston, Jamaica. More than a few of the passengers came back rather worse-for-wear after sampling the local brew and needed to be helped aboard. They put many a seaman to shame with the states they got into, but they caused more amusement than anything else.

At Havana in Cuba we were docked for a couple of days and I took the opportunity to go ashore with Bocker. The city was a very tense place and in the first bar we entered we were the only ones not carrying a gun. Although we didn't know it at the time, the Communist Revolution was less than five years away. If there was any trouble we wanted to be able to get off sharpish. As it turned out, we couldn't have been more wrong.

After a couple of drinks the ice was broken and we couldn't have wished to bump into a more decent bunch of lads. They were giving us the low-down on where to go and where not to go. In the end, we decided to stay where we were.

All was going well until a few of our boys who had been drinking heavily aboard ship came staggering in. They were full of the worst kind of mischief and looked intent on smashing the place up. I looked across at Bocker.

"This is all we bloody need!" I said, but for the second time I was wrong. As soon as they spotted the guns they changed their tune and within a minute everybody was shaking hands and buying each other a drink.

The owner of the bar was a giant Cuban. He was the size of John Wayne but a dead-ringer for his revolutionary leader, Fidel Castro. He wore a huge bushy beard and, standing up, his voice boomed across the bar.

"I have the greatest respect," he roared, "for the English!"

As you can imagine, this went down pretty well. He went on.

"Welcome to my bar, please enjoy yourselves ..." and then, tapping his gun on his hip and smiling broadly, "...or else!"

The boys went quiet for a moment and then the Cuban shouted out again. "Mary!" He looked at the woman behind the bar, "play some music and give these gentlemen a drink!"

To raucous cheers the music burst into life and everybody jumped to their feet dancing and jigging away. We had a great night but the Cuban wasn't daft. By the time we left we were

Tommy Miller

nearly all skint. On the way back we came across a big, dark-skinned woman sitting on a wooden box. She had thighs like an all-in wrestler on which she was rolling the finest Cuban cigars. I managed to scape together a few dollars and bought a few from her.

"When you return to your ship," she said, smiling seductively, "tell your friends the cigars you smoke were rolled on the thighs of a dusty maid!"

"Nice to meet you, dusty maid," I said, "my name's Dusty Miller!"

We left Havana the next day and headed south back across the Caribbean towards the beautiful Panama Canal, nearly as familiar to me now as the River Mersey. Sailing into the Pacific Ocean we called at Guayaquil in Ecuador and in the shadow of the Andes Mountains ran down the west coast of South America. We stopped for 'day excursions' at Callao and Pisco in Peru and Iquique and Antofagasta in Chile. Further down the Chilean coast we sailed into Valparaiso, or 'Valpo' as we called it, where we stayed for three days.

I hadn't seen much of Tony, my brother, since we'd left Liverpool. We were on different Watches and basically, he slept when I worked and vice-versa. He was the Plumber's Mate and I found him perched up a ladder, struggling with a spanner.

"Alright, Tony lad, how's tricks?" I asked.

"Oh, 'ello, Tommy!" He said. "I'm trying to fix this bloody thing."

142

"What's up?"

"There's a blockage in the sewage main. None of the toilets down this end of the ship are flushing. I've got to take this panel off and see if I can clear it. Trouble is, I don't think it's been taken off since the bloody ship was built! It's clogged up with rust and ten coats of paint!"

He'd managed to remove three of the corner bolts and was struggling and swearing at the fourth. I was about to bring up the subject of going for a drink when the bolt came free. The panel flew over his shoulder and the contents of every toilet pan at the bow end of the ship gushed over him. He slithered down the ladder and stood in front of me, silently dripping. I couldn't keep my face straight – but the best was yet to come.

The only way to the showers was past the passengers' accommodation, which promised to leave a smell they could all ponder over. He was about to sludge off when the old plumber, George, returned. He took a look at our Tony, saw the mess and hit the roof.

"Oh, Jesus Christ! What the bleedin' hell have yer done? Oh, this is bloody great, this is! Yer know, if yer want a bleedin' job doing properly, do it yer bleedin' ..." And just at that moment he slipped in the foul mess and went flying head over heels.

"Oh, Christ! Look at the bleedin' ..." Whoosh! Over he went again. The harder he tried to get on his feet, the more agitated he got and the more he slipped and slid around like a pissed-up roller-skater.

By the time I dragged myself away, I was in no fit state to tell anybody about it for twenty minutes. My side and cheeks were aching. I was sitting in the Mess trying to gather myself together and spit the story out to the lads when our Tony walked in. He was showered and changed and looked a lot better, but he wasn't very happy.

"That was all your fault, Tommy!" he said.

"My fault! How the hell do you make that out?"

"Yer distracted me! If yer hadn't been standing there jabbering away, it wouldn't have happened."

"Oh, well, never mind, Tony lad," I said, "you'll just have to consider yourself having been shit on from a great height!" And everybody was off again. We all had a right old laugh, and, to his credit, even old George, who wasn't exactly a laugh-a-minute, saw the funny side.

Chapter 19
Out of the Frying Pan

At 'Valpo' I went ashore with our kid, George and Bocker. I was back on duty at midnight with Bocker on the gangway, so we both decided to take it easy. Most seamen who made it to this part of the world would remember the 'Two Brothers' Bar'. They were world famous for their very special brew they called the 'Jug of Joy'. It was a type of punch containing just about every conceivable alcoholic drink. It was a lethal concoction. After a few glasses you were asking for a "Yuk of Yoy, plizz" and after a few more you were asking for a priest!

There was a story going round that when an English ship came in, the police let all the local thugs go free so they'd have enough cells for the drunken seamen. I wouldn't be surprised if it was true. Our reputation certainly went before us.

We enjoyed a few drinks, but at about eleven-thirty we left Tony and George and made our way back to the *Reina*. The two Q.M.'s who were waiting to stand down both had stories to tell.

One was Jack Morris, known as 'Solo'. He got his nickname during the war when, as a boy seaman on only his second trip, his ship was torpedoed in the Indian Ocean. Jack was the sole survivor. It must have been a terrifying experience but you'd never know what he'd been through just to talk to him.

The other lad was known as 'Beau Gest'. He was once docked in Marseilles and, having a few domestic problems back home, drowned his sorrows in the local bars and ended up in the 'nick'. By the time he got out, the ship had sailed without him and in the depths of despair he somehow talked himself into joining the Foreign Legion. Just how long he spent with them was a detail he didn't go into, but he got drunk again one night and did a runner. I suppose they've been looking for him ever since.

The next morning, half the ship's company was missing. Some had drifted off with local girlfriends, but the rest were filling the vacancies left by the local thugs. At breakfast the passengers had to serve themselves, probably a first for some of them. That day was Bocker's birthday and when we came off Watch we had a few beers in our cabin. I'd have been happy to stay put, but Bocker was all for going into town and as it was his birthday, that's where we went.

We dropped in on the 'Two Brothers' Bar' for a couple of 'Jugs of Joy' and then we headed for the 'Scandinavian Bar' or the 'Scandi' as it was known. The place was full of women and Bocker's eyes lit up.

"I can't see us leaving here before we have to!" he said. One of the reasons the 'Scandi' ws so popular with seamen was the way you could pay for your drinks. In Chili there was an acute shortage of metal and they were quite happy to take payment for half-a-dozen pints by way of a few knives and forks. It was no great mystery where the lads got the cutlery from. You'd see half-a-dozen lads walking down the street and if nothing else gave them away, you'd know they were seamen going to the 'Scandi' by the rattling in their pockets!

Another feature of the 'Scandi' was a local woman called Maria, who was one of the best dancers I ever saw. There's nothing remarkable about that in itself, except that Maria had a wooden leg! It was remarkable the way she could throw herself about and she also threw herself about in other ways which made her even more popular! A rum girl was Maria.

We ordered a drink and as we sat down two of the ship's engineers walked in. One of them was the starched shirt who'd had a run-in with one of the firemen, and true to form, the same fireman was standing at the bar. The engineer, a big enough lad, saw him straight away and made his way towards im. I thought he was going to shake his hand or buy him a drink, which would probably have been the best way to handle it. Instead, I nearly dropped my drink as he butted him square on the bridge of the nose. The fireman, a hard-case by anyone's reckoning, was taken completely by surprise and fell, pole-axed, to the floor. Within seconds all hell broke loose. It seemed all hands except me and Bocker were getting stuck in. There were bodies, chairs and bottles crashing all over the place. Bocker leaned towards me and had to shout to be heard above all the racket.

"Jesus, Dusty! We're due back in an hour, we'd better get out of here!"

"I'm right behind you, Bocker!"

The only way out of the bar was down a flight of about thirty steps. We both darted down the stairs and, before we realised it, straight into the back of a police wagon which had reversed up to the door of the club. The police gave us a right going-over. Apart from kicks and punches we got the full treatment of the batons, too. We were carted off to prison and thrown into a huge, hell-hole of a cell. Before long we had plenty of company. There were three 'gay' lads, as they'd be called nowadays, Sadie, Molly and Flo, aboard the ship and they were locked up, too. With little else to laugh about they kept us laughing with their camp antics and daft jokes.

"Excuse me, guard," said Sadie, "I think I've been booked into the wrong room, luvvie!"

The guard looked at him through the bars like he had two heads.

"It's just a teeny bit crowded in here, sweetie. If you check the reservations I think you'll find I'm sharing with you."

"Just a moment, dearest!" piped up Molly, "I saw him first, you tart!"

Fortunately, the guard didn't understand a word they were saying and left them to it.

They let us all go the following morning, but not before they'd relieved us of every dollar we carried. It was supposed to pay for the damage to the 'Scandi', but I doubt if one red cent ever got there. On the way out, Molly took hold of the guard by the arm and whispered in his ear loud enough for us all to hear.

"Next time, ducky, you can give me life!"

It was pretty busy outside the Captain's cabin as something like eighty men waited to be disciplined. I was more than a little bit peeved at being caught up in something I'd done my best to avoid, as was Bocker, but it was pointless trying to explain anything. Each head of the different departments was lined up with his cap under his arm calling each man in turn. Captain Whitehouse led the proceedings and everybody was dealt with the same.

"Second of September, 1954, absent without leave, fined ten shillings! Absent from duty, lose one day's pay! Get out! Next!"

With so many men to deal with there was no time and no need to elaborate. Each man passed through in seconds. When my turn came, he gave me a sharp glance.

"Miller! You are one of my quartermasters and you know I expect better! Ten shillings fine, lose a day's pay! Don't let me see you in front of me again. Get out!"

All the way home there were fights and squabbles. I was told she had a bad-tempered crew and I was told right. The butted fireman was determined to have his revenge and, predictably, before we got back to Liverpool, he did.

The engineer was pre-occupied for much of the journey home with a new girlfriend. She was a Cuban girl, a passenger on her way to an English university to study some 'ology' or other. You could sense they were growing more fond of each other as each day passed. A few days before we arrived back in Liverpool, I was coming off Watch just after midnight and I heard an unholy row going on between the two of them in his cabin. I'd got so used to them falling over each other I thought I must be hearing things, but there was no mistake.

"You feelthy Engleesh bastard! I hate you!"

As I passed the cabin door I could see her dragging him around by the hair. Blimey, I thought, love hurts! I got back to the Mess Room and started telling the lads, but it was already the topic of conversation.

"Been going on for half-an-hour," said 'Cabby' Furlong, "we thought someone was being murdered."

"I think there is!" I said. "What the bloody hell happened?"

"Ask him!" he said, pointing to the fireman who was quietly sitting at a table enjoying a smoke and a mug of tea. I'd got the feeling over the previous couple of days that we hadn't heard the last of the 'butting' incident and I thought he was cooking up something.

"What have you done?" I asked him.

"Nothing," he answered me, but his smug smile said otherwise. Bocker came up alongside me.

"Apparently somebody told the Cuban girl that her boyfriend was visiting the medic with a personal problem."

"What kind of personal problem?"

"The venereal disease kind!"

"Jesus! He's got VD!"

"Of course he hasn't, but she thinks he has!"

I looked down at the fireman whose smug smile had broadened into a huge grin.

"Couldn't happen to a nicer fella!" he said.

"Aye, this ship's full of nice fellas," I replied.

★ ★ ★ ★

It didn't matter what the engineer tried over the next few days, the romance was over. The fireman had known where to hurt him most. This was a strange ship but not without its lighter moments. The day after the break-up I was sitting in the Mess Room enjoying a mug of tea when the door flew open and one of the ship's barbers raced in. He was slightly unhinged at the best of times and was known, quite appropriately we all thought, as Sweeney Todd.

"I'm sick of life!" he screamed, "bloody sick of it!"

Everybody stopped what they were doing as he stormed around the Mess tables.

"I've had enough!" he blurted, "I'm going to do myself in!"

"Oh, shut up, you dope!" said Cabby.

"Have a cup of tea, Sweeney," Bocker offered.

"You're not listening, are you?" he carried on, "I'm gonna kill myself!"

"Well, make sure you do a good job," Bocker said, "'cause my solicitor's gonna be waiting for you at the Pier Head after the mess you made of my hair last week!"

We all had a laugh and, getting no sympathy, he disappeared back through the door.

A few minutes later the Bosun's mate came rushing in.

"Get up to Sweeny's cabin! There's some bloody strange noises coming from there!"

When we got there, Cabby put his shoulder to the door and it burst open. Inside, Sweeney was leaning over the sink, gurgling anf groaning, hacking at his throat with what appeared to be a piece of metal. The metal, it turned out, was the inside cover from a tin of tobacco and wasn't much more than a stiff piece of tin-foil. He obviously wasn't that intent in doing himself in!

"Bloody 'ell, Sweeney!" said Cabby. "if yer want the job doing properly, let me give yer a hand!"

At that, he pushed open a porthole, picked him up around the waist and made as if he was going to push him through. The screams were unmerciful.

"Argh! Put me down! Put me down! Argh! Murder! Murder! Help!"

In the end the whole thing broke down in hysterics. Sweeney managed to make it back to Liverpool in one piece, although I don't think he spoke to anyone. Needless to say, nobody asked him for a hair-cut. Years later, I heard that Sweeney had made himself a fortune with a chain of hairdressing shops in the south of

England. Life is full of surprises.

★ ★ ★ ★

We docked at Princes Landing Stage to disembark the passengers and as I approached the gangway there was my 'friend' the steward, waiting for his 'bloods'. To be fair, bloods is a term commonly used by stewards, but this one had a particularly cynical way of using it. I'd promised myself the last laugh at his expense and that was how it worked out.

As I stood by him, his eyes lit up as one of his bloods made her way towards him. She was a respectable looking lady in her sixties, immaculately dressed. She handed him an envelope and as she passed she thanked him for looking after her 'now and again', which she sarcastically emphasised. He opened up the envelope and pulled out a $5 bill. I thought that was a handsome tip, but he wasn't impressed.

"Miserable old bitch!" he muttered and put up two fingers behind her back. To one side, another of his bloods looked on. He was holding a bulging envelope which looked to contain some serious cash. He walked up to the steward and in a deep, American drawl said, "Well, son, I guess what you did to that lady you can do to me," and put the envelope back into his inside coat pocket. When he got to the bottom of the gangway, he turned back and stuck two fingers up at the steward before climbing into the same taxi as the $5 lady.

I couldn't help but laugh and that was reason enough for the steward to turn on me.

"You Scouse bastard!" he shouted. "I don't see what's so bloody funny!"

He raised his arms and started slapping and cuffing me around the head. My cap flew over the side of the ship and landed on the quay. He was a good fifteen years older than me so I didn't really want to hit him. I tried to calm him down but as he got more riled I had to grab him by the hair. The next thing, I was flat on my back, but the cause was in my right hand as I clutched onto his ragged toupe. His anger quickly evaporated into acute embarrassment.

"Go and get my cap," I told him, "and yer can have yer bloody wig back."

"Go and get it yerself!" he snapped hack.

I got to my feet smiling, walked towards him and plonked his hair-piece back into place.

"Next time you lose your temper," I suggested, "try and keep your hair on!"

There was a loud burst of laughter and I turned round to see 'Beau Geste' and half a dozen passengers enjoying the show.

I'd been warned about the *Reina Del Pacifico*. She wasn't a happy ship crew-wise and when I came ashore I vowed I'd never go back on her. Like a lot of things in life, though, saying and doing are not always the same.

Chapter 20
"Chewing the Bit"

I spent a fortnight at home and then signed up with the *M.V Sarmiento* under the same ownership as the *Reina Del Pacifico*. I was bound once again for the west coast of South America, but this time as an Able Seaman. It wasn't a case of being demoted or anything like that, but if you wanted regular trips you had to take what was available. So it was back to getting my hands dirty and working for a living; I was chipping the decks, painting the mast and painting the ship's sides.

There were usually four seamen to a cabin, but I was only sharing with two – a good mate called Jack Woodward from Bootle and Billy Shepherd. Jack wasn't a big lad, but he was built like a bull, and was the life and soul of the ship. He was madly in love with his "Sylvia" and would get really wound up if there wasn't a letter waiting for him whenever we docked. Thankfully, she thought the world of him, too, so that didn't happen very often.

Billy had done four trips on the *Sarmiento* and was a nice enough bloke, but he was forever scheming. When he came aboard he was humping along two massive hold-alls which he could hardly get up the gangway.

Jack shouted over to him, "Blimey, Billy! How long are you going away for – two years?"

"I always bring plenty of gear with me on this trip," he answered.

After a couple of days everybody began to notice a strong smell of perfume coming from our cabin. Jack turned to me,

"Bloomin' 'eck, Dusty, what are you wearing?"

"I was about to ask you the same," I said.

Billy piped up, "It's me. I like to wear a strong aftershave."

"Do us a favour, Billy!" I said, "who're you trying to impress?"

Another lad stuck his head in the doorway, "I'm fitting a red light outside here, you should do some good business!"

After we'd passed through the Panama Canal, the Captain, with his Chief Officer, Chief Engineer and Chief Steward, came below for their Sunday morning inspection of the cabins. They were all done up in their "go-ashore" uniforms. For a change, our cabin was spotless and all the bunks properly made. The Captain had a quick look around and then started sniffing.

"It smells like a brothel in here, Miller!" he said.

"I wouldn't know, Sir," I answered, "I've never been in one."

He looked at me with a wry grin and walked off chuckling.

At Valparaiso, we found the cause of the smell. Two well-dressed business men came on board and made their way to our cabin.

"How much have you got for us, then?" one of them asked Bill, who then pulled the two hold-alls, which were both filled with cosmetics, from under his bed. The two men seemed pleased – they gave Bill a roll of dollars and left with the bags.

I got talking to Bill and apparently they would only buy expensive perfume and it had to be Yardleys. For some reason the brand was very scarce in that part of the world and much sought after. He was paid about six times what he bought it for in Liverpool. He gave me and Jack $5 each.

"That's for putting up with the smell!" he said.

We hit the town and did the rounds of the usual bars, including the 'Scandi', which brought back memories. I had a dance with Maria and I marvelled again at the way she moved.

"I can't believe you've got a wooden leg!" I said to her.

"You can have a feel if you like," she answered, "but watch out for splinters!"

Homeward bound we had a different smell to put up with, carrying 600 tonnes of fish meal – we could have done with Bill's perfume then! One night we were having a few cans and reminiscing about different trips we'd been on. Bill Johnson, an old mate, said to me, "Remember the cock-up we made of burying that body?"

"Oh, don't remind me!" I said, "but it wasn't our fault. The bosun and his mate were too pissed to know what they were doing."

Our job had been to slide the body, wrapped in a canvas sheet, over the ship's side. On the day, the sea was like glass and the Captain ordered the engines to stop. All hands, and a few passengers, watched the ceremony. The body was wrapped in a union flag and Jack and myself held it on the rail. The Captain said a short prayer ending with the words "....I now commit this body to the deep." We gently slid the body over the side, and as it hit the water, it didn't sink. The body hadn't been weighted properly and we all watched in embarrassed silence as it bobbed along the sea's surface. The Captain, not a happy man, turned to his sheepish-looking Bosun.

"Can I have a word, please, Bosun," he said, and the two made their way to the Captain's cabin.

The Captain was called Jones and we went on to talk about him. He'd been Captain of the same ship for donkey's years and could be a right Captain Bligh in his day. When he finally died, he left a note in his will saying that he wanted his ashes scattered at sea at a particular place, giving the latitude and longitude specifications. This was duly arranged and the job was given to a senior apprentice officer.

Carrying a Bible and watched by the other apprentice Officers, he went to the ship's side. The new Captain ordered the engines to stop. At the time, we were busy painting the bulkheads in white gloss. We were just finishing what we were doing as the young officer was saying a prayer. I was just admiring my paintwork when suddenly it was covered with hundreds of black spots.

"Oh, bloody hell!" I shouted, "what's all this?" I thought it had come from the funnel, but when I turned round all the young officers were looking in my direction with horror-struck faces. Instead of throwing the casket over the side, the apprentice had taken the top off and scattered the ashes into the wind. The whole lot had blown over his head and stuck to the bulkhead. The young lad was mortified.

"Oh, my God. What am I going to do?" he gasped.

He started to make his way towards me.

"You'll have to scrape them all off!"

All the lads were having a chuckle at his expense. Nobody had much time for him.

"Made my day that," Jack said, "he's gonna be a right bastard when he gets his stripes."

The Bosun walked up to him, "If you think I'm having the men spend the next two days scraping up your mess," he said, "you can think again."

He looked over at me, "Dusty, paint over the ashes."

Which I duly did.

When the Captain found out he saw the funny side. "At least he's still with us," he said.

These stories had warmed everybody up and we were all having a good laugh. I turned to Bill Johnson again.

"Do you remember that fight in the Seven Steps, Bill?"

The Seven Steps was a well known pub on the Dock Road in Liverpool. "Bloody hell, I'll never forget it!"

The fight was between the dockers and the crew of the ship. We were about to sail on the *Mary Holt*. About eight of us were enjoying a quiet drink when a docker came over to our table.

"Do you wanna buy some barley sugar and condensed milk?" he said, and in his hands he was carrying a few packets and cartons. At the time our rations were only one carton of 'conny' every ten days, so we were always interested in any cheap extras.

Big Eddie Morris said, "Lets have a look, then." When he examined the carton, he saw, stamped on the side *Mary Holt.*

"What the hleedin' 'ell is this!" he shouted.

"What are you talking about?" the docker answered.

"This! Where the bleedin' 'ell did you get these from?"

"Never mind where I got them from? the docker answered back, "just give us a quid for the lot." The 'lot' had been stolen from our life boats.

Eddie got up and, without blinking, planted him square on the chin. He flew backwards and landed amongst about ten of his mates, all Freddie Mills lookalikes. There was ale and glasses all over the place, a sacrilege in any pub. The next thing, tables were turned over and stools were flying across the bar. The pub was rum by a manageress and her daughter and they were quickly on the scene and put a stop to it. It was amazing how burly dockers and seamen could be calmed down by a strong willed woman, although the threat of being barred from a pub was one the lads always took seriously. There was a few broken noses, including mine. It wasn't the first one I'd had. I remember in the Seaman's Mission in Buenos Aires I was talked into getting in the boxing ring. I was fighting the Padre, which I was quite happy about until I learned he was an ex-pro.

The dockers in the Seven Steps soon found out what had caused the trouble. Stealing from life-boats was against everybody's rules and they assured us the thief, and 'so-called' mate, would not work the docks again. Most dockers were ex-seamen themselves and they knew that it was the worst kind of crime to steal off each other.

This brings to mind the occasion when I was aboard a Liverpool liner and one seaman was caught stealing. We were twenty-four hours from home and most of us had been advanced a proportion of our pay. This was called 'Channel Money' or in Billy Shepherd's case, 'Channel N°9' Money. The stewards also had the cash they'd earned from their tips. Most of the lads kept their money in their lockers. The word had gone around that money had gone missing in Montreal, so we all knew there was a thief aboard.

In one particular steward's cabin, shared by eight men, there must have been quite a bit of cash around. Seven of them were up in the Pig and Whistle enjoying a good old sing-a-long before getting home. The other lad was the worse for wear after a few drinks and laying on his bunk. When the others returned they'd been back only a few seconds when all hell broke loose. Money had gone missing and old Joe, lying on his bunk was dragged up and called all the thieving bastards on earth. The lockers had been broken into and the thief obviously knew where to go.

"Hang on! Hang on!" screamed Joe, "when I was dozing somebody came in and I don't think he knew I was here! I was half asleep and half pissed I just thought he was fetching something!"

"Who was it then, Joe?" one of the lads shouted.

"It was Taylor!" he answered.

"It couldn't have been," said 'Chalky White', "he was with us!"

"Hold on a second." said Jim Nelson, "he did go missing for a bit, but I thought he'd gone the toilet."

"Taylor's got no reason for coming down here," said Chalky, "his cabin's on the starboard side. If Joe's right, what was he doing here?"

"Let's pay him a visit." said Jim, "no harm in asking him."

When they got to his cabin there was something of a party going on and Jim, quite casually, asked Taylor why he'd been in their cabin.

"I haven't been near your cabin." he said, "I was with you, what's the problem?"

"The problem is," said Jim, "our lockers have been broken into and a lot of hard-earned cash has gone missing. Just like in Montreal."

"Don't know anything about it," Taylor said, shrugging his shoulders."

Jim went on, "Old Joe reckons he saw you in our cabin."

"What does he know? He's always pissed."

The room went very quite and everybody listened to what was being said.

"You won't mind if we search your locker then?" said Jim, "or would you rather I fetched the M.A.?"

The M.A. was the Master at Arms.

"Help yourself," said Taylor, "I've nothing to hide."

Not surprisingly, nothing was found and Jim was about to apologise to Taylor when Chalky spotted a life jacket on top of Taylor's locker. What attracted his attention was the jacket was torn with the packing protruding from it. That is something you never see aboard ship. The Captains can be fined for such a lapse.

Chalky took down the lifejacket and he was made more suspicious by the haphazard stitching along the seams. With one pull Chalky opened the jacket and emptied the contents onto the cabin deck. Chalky separated what looked like a pile of cotton wool and there was all the missing money and a few other items that had gone missing.

"How do you know that's my life jacket?" screamed Taylor, "there's another seven like it in here!"

At that, his room mates turned on him and wanted to throw him overboard. There was pandemonium, but Chalky put a stop to it.

"Wait! Let's give this some thought!" he said, "if we throw him over the side it's murder! There's too many of us know about it. We'll all end up doing life."

"We can't let him get away with it, Chalky!" said Jim.

Taylor was obviously terrified and knew he was in for a bad time. As it happened, the justice served to him was severe and permanent, but I'll come back to that later.

Chapter 21
Take your Pick!

After leaving the *Sarmiento*, I signed on with the *Parthia* in June 1954. She was a 14,000 ton Cunard Line Cargo/Passenger Liner and a sister ship of the *Media*, which I sailed on twice a couple of years later. They were both on the Liverpool-New York run, but usually one would be arriving in New York as the other one was leaving. They were known as 'Intermediate Ships' in the Cunard Fleet, carrying about two hundred passengers. Generally, the cargo carried was a valuable one: Rolls Royce motor cars, Rolex watches, crates of select whisky and rum and cartons of expensive footwear. For most of us, walking around the hold was like a trip to Harrods! All dockers had at least one nickname in Liverpool and I remember one called "The Wonder Boy". He would poke around the different boxes saying "I wonder what's in this one? I wonder what's in that one?"

We docked at Pier 90 on New York's Hudson River. Pier 90 was only around the corner from the Merchant Navy Club on

51st Street and a couple of blocks away from Broadway and Times Square. It was a handy place to be docked. It also had its fair share of 'wonder' boys. The dockers there, or longshore men as they preferred to be called, began off-loading the ship. The following day, Johnny Riley, the bosun, sent Stan Jones and myself down into N° 1 Hold to remove some Lashing Wire from one of the tractors. When we'd finished, we were admiring some of the fancy motor cars when we noticed one of the Yankee dockers prizing the 'leaping czar' motif from a Jaguar car. I was about to go over and say something, but Stan stopped me.

"Leave it, Dusty, these fellas have a way of gettin' back at you."

Looking around we watched another docker tearing open a carton filled with boxes of shoes. The first one he opened revealed a beautiful suede pair, my favourites. The docker looked over at Stan.

"What size do you take, Limey?"

"Size eight, said Stan.

"There you go," said the Yank, "they'll cost you five dollars!"

"You must he bloody joking!" Stan said, "I can pinch them meself for nothing!"

"That's true!" The Yank nodded, "but I've got a better chance of getting them out of the hold."

This was true, too. He opened another carton and pulled out a box with "Hand-made Leather Shoes" printed on the side. When he opened it, his face broke into a broad smile. Inside was a tatty old pair of shoes. "Looks like one of your boys in Liverpool got to this one first!" he said.

This pilfering, or broaching of cargo as it was known, was rife and had a lot to do with the later introduction of containers. I remember the Ship Owners and the Insurance Companies coming up with a novel idea to stop the theft of shoes, which were very easy to pinch. They sent the left-footed shoes out on the Media and shipped out the right-footed shoes on the Parthia. They reasoned it was a good bet there wouldn't be many one-legged dockers either side of the Atlantic!

I parted company with the Cunard Line and signed on next with the Royal Mail Lines on the *S.S. Paraguay*. Once more I was bound for South America. We were busy loading the ship in Liverpool when the Hatch Boss called over to one of the dockers.

"Have you seen the Crab?" he shouted.

"No!" came the answer. I turned to a docker who was standing by me. "Who's the Crab?" I asked.

"Oh, that's Bill," he said. "We call him the Crab because every time we want him to work we have to tap him on the back."

I starred laughing, and having a receptive audience he warmed to his theme.

"Do you see that fella over there in the Army great coat, we call him the Coward. Since the day he got that coat it's had a big hole in it over his backside!"

Dockers nicknames are famous all over Liverpool and it was always good fun to listen to new ones.

"That fella there is the Lenient Judge." Most ships have guy ropes in constant use loading and off-loading. In order to trim the derrick you need to move the ropes around. The docker carried on.

"Every five minutes he's shouting 'let that guy go!' Hence the Lenient Judge."

I was having a right old chuckle at all this. "What about you?" I said to him.

"Oh, aye," he said, "we all have. They call me 'Fill the Pram'."

I chuckled. "Fill the Pram?"

"Yeah, well, last year my missus had twins and a couple of months ago she had another pair. You can see her pushing the pram up Scotland Road with four little heads bobbing up and down inside."

★ ★ ★ ★

I knew some of the lads on the *Paraguay* from previous trips. 'Booze' Bob Jones was the Second Cook. Anyone joining the ship who didn't know him would wonder where he got the name from, because he never touched the drink on board. Once he got ashore, though, he was a different beast altogether. Some of his 'boozing' exploits were legendary. I also knew two of the AB's, Frank Larson and Sid Moorcroft and one of the fireman, Ted Finnegan. Most of the lads down below on the *Paraguay* were in their fifties and knew the job backwards. They were all for the quite life, but they had done some serious galavanting in their time. They were all married now with grown up kids and they couldn't afford to carry on the way they used to.

We were on a two month trip and called into Bahia and Rio de Janeiro in Brazil and Motevideo in Uruguay. We stayed in each for a day or two, though there was little novelty in it for most of us. One lad had been on the Paraguay for two years and was known as the White Hunter. His particular racket was importing monkeys, snakes, parrots and tarantulas. We always said he carried more livestock than Chester Zoo! He had them planted all over the ship and at times you'd have thought we were in the middle of the Amazon Jungle when they all kicked off.

This brings back memories of a strange night on the *S.S. Zungeru* of the Elder Dempster Line. We left West Africa bound for Philadelphia with some general cargo and a few hundred live, caged monkeys. I was on the twelve-four watch on lookout on the head fo'c'sle. It was about half one in the morning when all hell broke loose. There were dozens and dozens of monkeys running wild over the deck. It was a beautiful moonlit night and looking up into the rigging I could see them leaping about having a fine old time. I never thought I'd see a monkey in the Crow's Nest!

The following day we caught most of them with the aid of a hose pipe, though a fair few fell into the sea. It's sad to say that they were probably the lucky ones as the rest were to be used for live experiments on a whole host of things. It turned out that one of the lads had felt sorry for them and released them all, but nothing was ever proven. This was a regular cargo for the Zungeru even the Captain was known as 'Monkey' Williams.

Our next port on the Paraguay was Buenos Aires. The lads

who hadn't been there before were warned by those of us who had to be careful with the local police. "Don't even look sideways at them!" they were told. We knew from experience they enjoyed few things more than humiliating English sailors and, like the Flying Flea, have them brushing the streets or picking up litter in the parks. Most of us decided to stay on board.

We bought a few cases of cans from the Chief Steward and after a few everybody was loosening up. All the musical instruments came out including a guitar, and a harmonica, or as we called it 'a gobiron'. There were castanets and, more unusual, a flute. When the lad on the flute started up we couldn't believe it.

"Bloody hell, Jim!" I said, after he'd finished one tune. "What are you doing working on this crate when you can play like that. You should be in the Philharmonic Orchestra!"

"Oh, it's just a hobby," he said, happy with the compliment but very modest about it, "I'm not that good."

One of the lads told a joke about a Liverpool seaman signing up with a new ship. The Bosun, from Surrey took an instant dislike to him and told the Captain.

"I've no time for bloody Scousers!" he said.

"Why's that, then?" said the Captain.

"Because you can't trust them. They'll rob anything."

Once the ship was at sea, the Scouser was working on deck with a mop and bucket, giving the deck a good wash down. Suddenly, a massive wave hit the ship and swept the Scouser, mop and bucket over the side. They never saw him again.

"I told you!" the Bosun said to the Captain, "that bleedin' Scouser has pissed off with the mop and bucket!"

The two lads who had gone ashore met with no problems and were telling us about the two 'senoritas' they had met and spent the night with. Dick Bloomfield, who had worked the South American coast for years, asked Kevin, one of the lads, where they met them.

"In May Sullivan's Bar," he answered.

"What were their names?"

They told him and while we all gave knowing looks to each other, Dick came straight to the point.

"Those two have got the clap up to their eyelids!" he said.

The other lad, Paul, stood up. "I don't believe it!" he said, "she told me she was clean!"

"Aye," said Dick, "she told me and a dozen others the same. We all went home with a packet."

While we were in Buenos Aires, on board ship having our dinner, this chap came into the Mess Room. He looked like a typical Argentine until he opened his mouth from which a thick Scouse accent emerged.

"Everythin' alright, fellas?" he said cheerily.

It turned out he'd been 'on the beach' for about twelve years, a phrase given to those who miss their ship through being locked up, hospitalised or whatever and are left stranded. More officially they are known as 'distressed seamen' and he would board most English ships in port and be given a square meal and a bunk for the night. He was well known and quite popular with the lads who made this trip regularly. He had been out there that long he was known as 'Senor Cairnes'.

Apparently, he'd spent most of his life at sea and the story went that he and a mate had beaten up a ship's Chief Engineer to within an inch of his life when they were in Buenos Aires. Knowing they faced a lengthy prison sentence, and worse if he died, the both absconded. They decided to stay in Argentina knowing they would be arrested if they ever went back to England. A few days out of Liverpool, Kevin and Paul were both looking decidedly worried. Dick asked them, already knowing what was up.

"Well, you were right about that bleedin' senorita!" Kevin said, "but that's only part of my problem. I'm supposed to be gettin' married when I get home!"

"You certainly have got a problem!" said Dick, "but this is what you'll have to do. When we dock, go and get treated straight away, then go straight to the Seamen's Pool and get yourself a ship going away for a few months. Make any excuse to cancel the wedding. Just say you want to get married in style, or whatever, but get yourself out of the way until you're in the clear."

It was years later before I sailed with Kevin again and found out what happened.

Chapter 22
The 'San Cirilo' Disaster

I left the *Paraguay* and decided I'd deserved a break and spent the best part of six weeks at home. I'd started courting Frances by this time, who later became, and still is, my wife. I was keen to spend a bit more time at home. It was during this break that I was home one night flicking through the pages of the Liverpool Echo when my attention was caught by a headline that shook me to the roots.

The Liverpool Echo   Wednesday 13th April 1955

EIGHT MEN KILLED AND OTHERS INJURED IN BRITISH TANKER EXPLOSION

The 13,896 ton Argentine tanker 'Juvenal' radioed during the night that she was going to the aid of the drifting British tanker 'San Cirilo', the boiler of which had exploded and killed eight of the crew. Several of their men were injured, the message said.

The 8,045 'San Cirilo', owned by Eagle Oil and Shipping Company, of London, gave her position as 5 degrees 20 minutes north, 45 degrees 12 seconds west, the Juvenal stated. This is about 500 miles east of Cayenne, French Guinea. Captain Dudley W. Mason, G.C., Superintentent [sic] to the Company, said in London today: "We are asking for double confirmation on casualties. A statment may be made later."

SHIP ALONGSIDE

A passenger vessel was reported to be alongside the 'San Cirilo'. Shell Mex in Argentina, agents for the 8,045 ton tanker, said they understood the unidentified passenger ship had replaced the Juvenal. The 'San Cirilo' had a crew of about 40 and is commanded by Captain M. E. Holdron, M.B.E. Latest reports said she had now drifted south to a point north-east of the mouth of the Amazon River. The 'San Cirilo' was carrying petroleum from Dutch Aruba in the Caribbean to Buenos Aires - Reuter.

I'd spent more than two months on the *San Cirilo* up to Christmas Day, 1952. My first thoughts were that there was every chance I knew one or two of the men who had been killed. My mate, Mick O'Shaughnessy, who had thumped the Bosun, had left her the same time as I had, but there were others who may have still been with her.

Although whenever anything like this happened it was a shock to the system, I can't say that I was surprised it had happened to the *San Cirilo*. I'd never known a ship to spend so much time at sea broken down. The following day I bought the Echo as soon as it hit the shops and the news was worse.

The Liverpool Echo   *Thursday 14th April 1955*

SHIP BLAST DEATH ROLL NOW ELEVEN INJURED LIVERPOOL MAN DIES

Three men injured in the boiler explosion in the tanker 'San Cirilo' (8,045 tons) have died, it was learned in London today, making a total of eleven deaths.

One of the men was Fireman K. Hunter [sic], of Windsor Street, Liverpool. This brings the total of victims from Liverpool up to four. Mrs. John Hunt, the mother of Fireman Hunt, said this afternoon that her boy sailed aboard the 'San Cirilo' because he had missed the ship he intended to sail with. He was given an hours notice to get ready at the time and it sailed without him.

Fireman Hunt, who was 20, joined the Merchant Navy at Christmas after being in the Army for 3 years. He first sailed in a Canadian vessel for three weeks and had been five weeks in the 'San Cirilo' to the day when the accident happened. He was one of ten children of Mr. and Mrs. Hunt, who were yesterday notified that their son had been severely burned in the explosion. This morning they were informed of his death.

The 'San Cirilo' was carrying crude oil from Aruba to Buenos Aires. She had a crew of 46. The explosion occurred on Tuesday, when the 'San Cirilo' was off South America.

Captain Dudley W. Mason, G.C., Marine Superintendent of the owners Eagle Oil and Shipping Company Ltd., of Finsbury Circus, London, E.C., told a reporter that he had learned today of the deaths of three men who were yesterday reported injured.

IN ARGENTINE SHIP

Fireman Hunt was on board the Argentine ship Rio Tercero, which was taking him to Trinidad. The other two injured men died on board the 'San Cirilo' before the 'Rio Tercero', who had a doctor on board, could reach her.

They were Junior Engineer A. J. Rose of Maberley Street, Aberdeen and Deck Boy J. Dickens of Rushden, Northants. Captain Mason stated that several other ships were in the vicinity of the 'San Cirilo' and some engineer assistance had been obtained. It was hoped she would be escorted by a ship to Trinidad for repairs.

KEEN ATHLETE

The three Liverpool men previously reported killed were Junior Engineer Ronald John Dutton, aged 22, eldest son of Mr. & Mrs. John Dutton, of 134 Marina Crescent, Netherton; Fireman J. Grainger. aged 23, of Marsham Way, Liverpool 11; and Greaser J.

Hollingshead, aged 29, of 42 Haddock Street, Liverpool 20.

Junior Engineer Dutton was a keen athlete, having won the 1951 trophy for being the outstanding athlete in The Liverpool Boys Association. Twelve months ago he completed an engineering apprenticeship and joined the Eagle Oil and Shipping Company, owners of the San Cirilo. This was his second trip in the tanker.

PARTY PREPARATIONS

Fireman Grainger's parents, Mr. & Mrs. W. Grainger, were preparing a re-union party for him and his brother Jimmy, when news of the tragedy was received. Fireman Grainger had been at sea only about one year.

Greaser Hollingshead had been at sea since he was 17½, when he joined the Royal Navy. He entered the Merchant Navy after the war. He lived with his grandmother. Mrs. Margaret Hollingshead, both his parents being dead.

The style of reporting all seems very dated now, but it still made very depressing reading at the time. As it happened I did not know any of the lads who had died, but over the next few days I spoke to mates who did. Like myself they were all in their twenties, just doing a job of work and wanting to see the world. It was very sad.

Chapter 23
"Bugs"

Back in 1947 I had stood on the dockside at Montreal gazing open-mouthed at the impressive size of the *Empress of Scotland*. Now, more than eight years later, I signed on with the Canadian Pacific Company and joined her for the first time. I was surprised to learn she was the largest ship in the world to enter Montreal and in order to pass under the Quebec Bridge her masts had been shortened by forty-five feet.

By this time, I was making wedding plans with Frances and we were talking about naming the day towards the end of the year. I was keen to spend more time at home and as the Montreal run was little more than a four week round-trip, it suited me fine. My galavanting days were over and it was time to start putting some money away.

"How many trips are you thinking of doing on her, Dusty?" the Bosun asked me.

"Eleven," I said.

"Eleven?" he answered, "that's very precise. Are you thinking of settling down then?"

"No." I said, holding up one finger of each hand, "eleven to me is one trip out and one home!"

On joining a ship this size it was inevitable that I would meet with someone I'd sailed with before and, good enough, it wasn't long before I bumped into my old mate, Bill Rice. I'd last sailed with Bill a couple of years earlier on a run-job aboard the *British Supremacy*, the first ship I'd joined after leaving the *San Cirilo*.

I was also with him on board the *Derryheen* when as a young lad I had circumnavigated the globe, and he reminded me of a 'joint' we had visited in Singapore called Toby's Paradise Bar.

"Did you ever go for a drink anywhere in the world in a place with such an inappropriate name?" asked Bill.

"No, I don't think so," I chuckled back. The bar had more blood on the walls and ceilings than an abattoir. I remember sitting in there one afternoon having a quiet drink with Bill and a couple of other lads, when we were approached by a Yank.

"Do you guys wanna fight?" he said.

"No, thanks," we told him.

"OK", he said walking off, "if that's the way you want it, I'll go find somebody who does!"

"Do you remember that run down to Falmouth, Dusty?" asked Bill.

"Not 'alf!" I replied, "On the *British Supremacy*. I'm still bloody scratching from that crate!"

Bill turned to some of the other lads who were listening and laughing.

"Me and Dusty signed on with this tanker running down to the south coast from Ellesmere Port. She docked on the Monday and sailed on the Tuesday. I'm telling you, she turned around that fast the last crew had left a pot of tea and it was still warm when we boarded! Anyway, when we gets to our cabin the linen from the last lot hasn't been changed and we had to get into our bunks without fresh sheets. For the next six hours nobody got a wink of sleep. We were all itching and scratching and tossing and swearing. Dusty here, switches on his bunk light and on the pale cream of the bulkhead all you could see was a grey mass of king-size bugs!"

"That's right!" I added, "bloody great huge things!"

I went on to tell the lads how the next morning we'd gone to see the Chief Officer. He spoke so far back he was in the next country.

"Bags!" he said, "bags! I don't believe it! You Scousers must have brought them with you!"

That is an awful insult to seamen who go to a lot of trouble to maintain cleanliness. I've known some lads to tie a man to a mast and hose him down because he didn't wash often enough.

I told the Chief Officer that if he didn't have the ship fumigated in Falmouth he'd lose his crew.

"It's very expensive fumigating a ship," he said, "and, in any case, she's probably going into dry dock in Falmouth and you will all be paid off. You will have to put up with your 'bags'."

As he turned away he grinned sarcastically. I weighed him up and decided I'd plan something for this fella before I left the ship. The next day we were cleaning down the hold's tank until midnight, and it was hard going. When we were finished the Chief officer gave us each a double rum, saying, "Here you are, Miller, get this down you and you won't be worrying about any bags!"

Oh, I thought, I'll have you sunshine, I'll have you. After the shot of rum, the Chief turned to me, seeing me by this time, I suppose, as a kind of ringleader.

"By the way, Miller, if you go to the galley, the Cook has kindly left out some food for you. As it's so late, I'm afraid you'll have to cook it yourselves."

We were so hungry, we didn't mind that one bit. When we got there, the cook had left us a tray of two dozen sausages and nothing else. No bread, no potatoes, nothing. On closer examination, the sausages were beginning to go green with mould and seemed to be inching their way to the side of the tray.

There being nothing else, we decided to cook them. I'd often wondered why sausages were called 'bangers' and here was the answer as they spat and popped under the grill.

"Sounds like machine gun fire!" said Bill. It was that bad we stood by with a fire extinguisher.

"It's not a fire extinguisher we need!" I said, "it's the bloody fire brigade!"

I was made the Chief Sausage Cook, but I could do little to make them appetising. When I served them up I was the first to admit they looked disgusting. Out of sheer hunger one of the lads began to eat them, but when he was on the third, he stood up sharply and dashed out of the mess to be sick.

We'd had enough and went up onto the bridge and knocked on the Captain's door. As it was by now two thirty in the morning, it didn't put him in the best of moods. We challenged him to taste one. Taking a bite, he turned it around in his mouth, grimacing before he swallowed. After choking back a look of disgust, he said.

"My God, that was beautiful! Take them away before I eat them all!" and promptly slammed his door in our face. Even though we were all starving, we all thought this exhibition of stubborness was funny.

The following day we were in Falmouth and were being paid-off. While we were being made to wait for our money, I went down to our cabin and filled two matchboxes with the bed-bunks. The Captain and Chief Officer were on deck talking ship's business, so after making sure nobody was about I went into the Chief's cabin and emptied the contents of one of the boxes under the lower sheet of his bunk. I then did the same in the Captain's cabin.

To this, I admit, but I had nothing to do with the left over sausages being stuffed into the Captain's socks and it wasn't me who put Epsom salts in the Officers' soup!

As I was leaving the ship, making my way down the gangway, the Chief Officer called after me.

"I hope you've taken your 'bags' with you, Miller!"

"Don't worry, sir!" I shouted back. "We've left a couple for you!"

The *Empress of Scotland* was a huge, impersonal ship, and much of an uninteresting voyage was passed in this way, going over old stories. We got back to Liverpool on 24th May, 1955, but I was keen to earn as much cash as I could now I was making wedding plans and three days later I was bound for the Persian Gulf aboard the *M.V. El Mirlo*.

Chapter 24
"He's drunk the compass dry, sir!"

The *El Mirlo*, an old tub of a ship, was owned by Bowrings & Co. and must have been forty years old when I boarded her. As it happened, the ship suited my wedding plans because I was able to save some money. Each seaman was allowed only two cans of beer a day, so most of us didn't bother. Instead, we decided to become keep-fit fanatics and held competitions to see who could do the most press-ups and such. I'd thought I was as fit as the next man until I started on the physical jerks!

One night the shortage of ale had one of the lads talking about a 'dry' ship he'd been on. The Captain and his officers were totally against any alcohol being aboard ship.

"If you're thirsty," the Captain would say, "you can have all the lime juice and pots of tea you like!"

One morning the old man noticed one of the hands staggering along the deck. After watching him for a few moments, he instructed the Bosun to have the man brought up to the bridge.

When he arrived, no alcohol could be smelt on his breath.

"We are in perfectly good weather, Lafferty," the Captain said to him, "the ship is not rolling and yet you were staggering around the deck like a drunkard. Can you explain yourself?"

"Yes, sir," said Lafferty.

"Then please do."

"Vertigo, Sir."

"Vertigo?"

"Yes, sir. I suffer from bouts of vertigo."

"Good heavens!" the Captain exclaimed, "I had no idea!"

He turned to his Chief Officer. "Do you know my aunt suffers from vertigo?"

"Really, sir," replied the Chief sardonically.

"Indeed yes! Quite badly, in fact. I remember one occasion a few years ago, she stumbled quite badly because of it and very nearly fell under a bus! Terrible business!"

"It must have been, sir."

The Chief Officer was no great admirer of Able Seaman Lafferty and was quite sceptical about the whole performance. Turning toward the Chief, the Captain went on.

"I am holding you personally responsible for this man. I don't want to see him working up the ship's masts or at any height. In fact I want him put on very light duties!"

"Yes, sir."

By the time they arrived in port, his condition had, if anything, got worse and he was admitted to hospital. A day or two later he was diagnosed as suffering from alcoholic poisoning. Apart from his embarrassment at being so gullible, the Captain was astounded.

"That's impossible! There's not one drop of the stuff on my ship!" he said.

The lad telling the story told us that all the lads were baffled, too. If somebody is having a sly drink aboard a dry ship, his mates soon find out where it's coming from. Yet nobody had seen a thing.

The ship left port without Lafferty and the mystery remained a mystery. About a week later there was a lifeboat drill. The covers were taken off and each boat was swung out and lowered a few feet. All went well, so each boat was brought back in board and re-covered. At that moment the Bosun noticed the lifeboat compass was lying on its side. He climbed out to put it back and noticed the Compass Card was bone dry. He called for the Chief Officer.

"What's the problem?" he said, arriving a minute later.

"The Compass Card," said the Bosun, "it's bone dry!"

The Chief climbed out onto the Lifeboat and knelt down next to the Bosun.

"No alcohol!" he said.

"Not a bloody drop, sir." The Chief looked at the Bosun, "Are you thinking what I'm thinking?" he said.

"Lafferty!" exclaimed the Bosun. They checked the cards on

the other three compasses on the ship and found them in a similar condition.

"How the hell could he drink pure bloody alcohol?" said the Chief.

"Lime juice!" answered the Bosun, "everytime I looked at him he was drinking bloody lime juice! He was mixing it!"

I did a second trip on the *El Mirlo* and all was going according to plan for the wedding. Homeward bound, we stopped off at Bordeaux, along the Garonne River on the French Atlantic coast and Rouen, up the River Seine from Le Havre. We dropped part cargoes of oil then, as I thought, we were setting off for home.

In port at Rouell, the Chief Officer approached me. "What date are you getting married, Miller?"

"26th December, sir," I replied. "Boxing Day".

"You'll have to forget about it, then." he said.

"What are you talking about?"

"We're not going home, we are turning straight round and bound again for the Gulf. You won't be home until January."

"What!" I shouted, "who the bleedin' hell dreamt that up?"

"Sorry, Miller, it's out of my hands."

He was quite right, of course. The decision was nothing to do with him, but that didn't stop me calling him all the names under the sun. After I'd blown steam for a few minutes I had to accept the wedding was, temporarily, off. Just like Eric Jones on the *Derryheen* eight years earlier, I had to take it on the chin.

I decided not to write to Frances, but to send her a telegraph once we'd put to sea. She's going to love this, I thought.

We made our way up the Garonne River, bound for the open sea and the Persian Gulf. I was on deck and feeling thoroughly miserable when I noticed a ship closing in on our port side. "She's cutting it fine, isn't she" I shouted out, and the lads round about looked up to watch. She drew nearer and seemed to be making no attempt to avoid us. The impending danger hadn't gone unnoticed on the bridge and suddenly a shout went up.

"Hard a-starboard! Full astern!"

It was too late. In an effort to avoid the other ship's course, we hit a solid concrete jetty on the starboard side. The ship's bows caved in.

After the excitement had settled down we put back into port. An interesting argument broke out between the Captain, who wanted to take the ship onto the Gulf and the Chief Officer, who said the ship wasn't fit to go anywhere but home for repairs. The Captain always had the last word, but he also knew the Chief had the backing of the men regarding whether or not she was seaworthy. Reluctantly, the Captain had the hole plugged with concrete and we limped back across the Channel.

Fortunately for myself and Frances, this meant the wedding was back on again and once in Liverpool I had time for one more trip and another wage packet before the 'big day'.

Chapter 25
My Final Fling

I was looking for a ship were the possibilities of being re-directed were very limited, and after being home just a few days I signed on the *Arabia*, a cargo ship belonging to the Cunard Line. She was on the Liverpool-New York run and I'd sailed on her sister ship, the *Assyria*, three years earlier.

The Deck Department, as the ABs were known, have to familiarise themselves with the working rig of each ship they join. This can take a few days, but as the *Arabia* was identical to the *Assyria*, I had no such problems. While we were off-loading in New York I was given a reminder of the time of the year.

"Take a look at this, Dusty," said John Foy, one of the ABs. Looking down the ship's hold, there must have been about four tons of Christmas Puddings, made by a Liverpool bakery and now exported to the States.

We went ashore and for myself it was a final fling as a single man. We went across the bridge to Brooklyn and were enjoying the bars. In one we were served by a midget. He was only about four foot six, but he had the broadest shoulders I've ever seen on a man his size. One of the lads, Gerry from Blackpool, decided to be a smart-alec and said to the barman, "I tell you what, I wouldn't mind taking you home for Christmas for the kids to play with!"

Without saying a word, the man came from behind the bar, put Gerry, a big man, in an arm lock and ran him from one end of the bar to the other, flinging him through the door and into the street. Dusting himself down, he returned behind the bar and look at the rest of us.

"Any more comments before I serve you?" he said, in a thick New York drawl. We shook our heads and muttered comments to the effect that we would be as good as gold. Needless to say, big Gerry never lived that down. I remember on one occasion, one of the lads was having some bother with an ex-boyfriend of his fiancée.

"How big is this fella?" I said.

"Oh, he's only about five foot two," he answered.

"Too big for Gerry to sort out for you, then!"

Chapter 26
An End and a Beginning

I married Frances on the afternoon of Boxing Day, 1955 at St. Philomena's R.C. Church in Sparrow Hall. The weather was miserable, but we could expect little else in the middle of the winter. At least the 'do' that night, at the Old Pirie Labour Club, was free of the usual wedding fights and scraps.

In those days a honeymoon was a rare luxury and four days later I had to kiss my bride goodbye and join my ship. There was novelty in this trip as I had to fly to Holland to pick the ship up in Rotterdam. For most of us, including myself, it was the first time we had flown. We were picked up by a coach, or a charabanc as we used to call them, and taken to Speke Airport. Our gear was 'off-loaded' onto the tarmac and we stood by admiring the beautiful Boeing jet which taxied toward us. We were all a bag of nerves in truth, but we joked around like big kids.

"I'm sitting by the window, miss!"

"I'm having the back seat!"

I'd drunk that much rum to settle my nerves, I would have been happy in the luggage department! Much to our surprise and disappointment, the Boeing glided past us and took off, reveaing an old crate of a DC-10 Dakota.

"Look at the state of that!" said one lad, "I bet you Douglas-Baader's the bloody pilot!"

"I'm not saying it's old," said another, "but isn't that an outside toilet?"

"Jump on me shoulders, and crank the handle!"

All this seems a bit dated now, but this was the first time I'd heard some of these cracks. The lads were no better once we'd boarded. The stewardess was a young, Liverpool girl and, if I remember correctly, her name was Betty Gillon. She certainly had her hands full.

"Eh, Betty!"

"What's the matter?"

"Ask the driver if he can pull up at the next alehouse!"

"I bet the beer's like rocket fuel!"

"Give us a song, Betty!"

This was cue enough for one of us to burst into song and we all joined in.

"Oh, I do like to be beside the seaside!
Oh, I do like to be beside the sea!
Oh, I do like to be beside the prom, prom prom!
Where the brass band plays Tiddly-om-tom-tom!"

We were each supplied with a carton for our so called 'in-flight' meal. The lads tucked into an assortment of pies, cold meat and sandwiches, but when I opened mine the box was empty.

"What's going on here, Betty?"

"Oh, hang on a minute," she said. "I'll see if I can find a spare one." She was back in two minutes. "Here, the Captain said you can have his."

"Eh," said Charlie Connor, sitting next to me, "does this mean I'm sitting at the Captain's Table, Dusty?"

"Be the first and last time, Charlie!" The banter carried on.

"Eh, Betty! I'm not very happy about me parachute!" said Johnny Finnigan, waving his sick bag.

"Nip down the back, Betty, and make sure we've got enough lazzy bands to get us there!"

We flew at 900 feet and travelled at 120 knots and by the time we put down two and a half hours later at Amsterdam's Schiphol Airport, Betty, who stayed in good humour throughout, was probably glad to see the back of us.

We were driven down to Rotterdam and joined the *S.S. Beaverlodge*, belonging to the Canadian Pacific Steamship Co. who I'd sailed with before on the *Beaverburn*.

We were bound for Montreal, something of a sentimental journey for me, although I made it often enough. I was always reminded of my first trip with our John and 'Nutty' on the *Empire McDermott*. On board, one crew member I recall was Tony Oldham. It was Tony who, during one of the seamen's strikes, was one of the first to stand up and say we should get back to work. It didn't make him very popular at the time, hut I remember admiring him for having the strength of his convictions. He was also a useful boxer in his day and I suppose that helped. He later became a delegate for the Seaman's Union (NSU), and nobody ever doubted he said what he thought.

Approaching Montreal, we passed the Strait of Belle Isle and picked up the Pilot at Father Point. We entered the St Lawrence River "of a thousand churches" and passed again the beautiful Chateau Frontenac! Past Quebec onto Montreal, we off-loaded, and sailed for home.

A few days later I was back in Liverpool with Mrs Miller. After a week finances directed me back to work and I joined the Scythia, heading once again for North America.

Tommy Miller's Sea Voyages

Vessel	Sign-Up	Discharge	Destinations
Empire McDermott	02.03.47	09.04.47	Canada
Empire McDermott	19.04.47	30.05.47	Canada
Derryheen	07.06.47	19.03.48	USA, Australasia, Fiji
Inventor	10.04.48	30.06.48	W.Indies, Venezuela, USA
Fort Musquarro	07.07.48	07.09.48	USA
Fort Musquarro	14.09.48	30.10.48	USA
Fort Musquarro	02.11.48	27.01.49	USA
Bantria	19.02.49	15.04.49	Gibralta, Greece, Turkey
Bantria	21.04.49	27.04.49	Gibralta, Greece, Turkey
Bantria	05.05.49	09.07.49	Gibralta, Greece, Turkey
Beaverburn	20.07.49	13.08.49	Canada
Beaverburn	23.08.49	16.09.49	Canada
Beaverburn	24.09.49	17.10.49	Canada
Beaverburn	24.10.49	23.11.49	Canada
Esso London	06.12.49	23.01.50	Iran
Zungeru	31.01.50	27.04.50	Canary Isles, W.Africa
Alca	06.05.50	23.07.50	Canary Isles
Potaro	05.08.50	05.11.50	Brazil, Ureguay, Paraguay
Debrett	20.11.50	07.02.51	S.America
Denbigh Coast	15.02.51	23.02.51	Wales
Denbigh Coast	24.02.51	28.02.51	Wales
Cabano	14.03.51	10.09.51	W.Coast Africa

Vessel	Sign–Up	Discharge	Destinations
Mary Kingsley	11.10.51	02.01.52	W.Coast Africa
Assyria	27.08.52	21.09.52	USA
San Cirilo	16.10.52	25.12.52	Persian Gulf
British Supremacy	08.01.53	21.01.53	Cornwall (UK)
City of Cardiff	27.01.53	17.02.53	Hull (UK)
Smaria	27.02.53	10.07.53	USA
Samaria	11.07.53	16.12.53	USA
Reina Del Pacifico	08.02.54	14.03.54	S.America, Bermuda
Sarmiento	26.03.54	18.06.54	S.America, Bermuda
Parthia	24.06.54	14.08.54	USA
Parthia	15.08.54	04.12.54	USA
Paraguay	14.12.54	17.03.55	Paraguay
Empress of Scotland	06.05.55	24.05.55	Canada
El Mirlo	27.05.55	24.07.55	Persian Gulf
El Mirlo	25.07.55	22.11.55	Persian Gulf
Arabia	16.11.55	15.12.55	USA
Beaverlodge	30.12.55	14.02.56	Canada
Scythia	22.02.56	18.03.56	USA, Canada
Florian	24.03.56	12.05.56	Mediterranean
Franconia	18.05.56	10.06.56	USA
Nova Scotia	20.06.56	20.08.56	Canada, USA
Carinthia	27.08.56	06.10.56	USA
Hyala	14.10.56	23.10.56	Home Trade
Media	27.10.56	17.11.56	Canada, USA
Media	18.11.56	05.12.56	Canada, USA
Accra	28.12.56	30.01.57	W.Africa
Tamele	11.02.57	07.04.57	W.Africa
Hemsley	18.04.57	08.05.57	Mersey Estuary (UK)
Reina del Pacifico	21.05.57	24.07.57	W.Coast S.Am. (W.Coast)
Scythia	08.08.57	22.12.57	USA
Imperial Star	10.01.58	20.06.58	Australasia, Pitcairn Islands
Dunadd	10.07.58	12.08.58	Canada
Maltecian	19.08.58	22.10.58	Mediterranean
Reina Del Mar	05.10.58	13.01.59	S.America (West Coast)

Vessel	Sign-Up	Discharge	Destinations
Elmol	10.01.59	04.02.59	Home Trade
Empire Gaelic	16.02.59	21.02.59	Ireland
Media	24.02.59	16.05.59	USA
Media	17.05.59	13.06.59	USA
Britannic	25.06.59	20.07.59	USA
Changuinola	01.08.59	26.08.59	Tiko (West Indies)
Obopo Palm	08.09.59	07.11.59	W.Africa
Nova Scotia	02.12.59	13.03.60	Canada, Newfoundland
Sylvania	23.03.60	16.04.60	USA
Empire Nordic	27.04.60	30.04.60	Ireland
Flaminian	06.06.60	13.06.60	Mediterranean
Flaminian	20.06.60	03.08.60	Mediterranean
Andania	28.09.60	18.10.60	Home Trade
Zent	01.11.60	04.12.60	W.Indies
Zent	13.12.60	04.02.61	W.Indies
Zent	08.02.61	15.03.61	W.Indies
Mary Holt	22.03.61	28.04.61	Home Trade
Zent	17.05.61	DNS	- -
Anselm	26.05.61	31.05.61	Holland - Liverpool
Coptic	03.06.61	05.06.61	Home Trade
Tewkesbury	07.07.61	DNS	Home Trade
Crystal Dimaond	21.06.61	03.09.61	S.Africa
Arabia	22.09.61	15.10.61	USA
Arabia	17.11.61	13.12.61	USA
Sylvania	21.12.61	07.03.62	USA
Oremina	14.03.62	19.04.62	S.America
Empress of Canada	01.05.62	18.05.62	Canada
Accra	24.05.62	25.06.62	W.Africa
Nova Scotia	03.07.62	07.08.62	Canada
Venetian	17.08.62	DNS	- -
Pizarro	08.09.62	02.10.62	S.America
Ocean Transport	09.10.62	11.10.62	Home Trade
Reina Del Mar	22.10.62	20.12.62	S.America
Chuscal	27.03.63	21.04.63	W.Indies

Vessel	Sign-Up	Discharge	Destinations
Beechmore	27.04.63	31.05.63	Canada, Newfoundland
Beechmore	06.06.63	09.07.63	Canada, Newfoundland
Beechmore	16.07.63	19.08.63	Canada, Newfoundland
Beechmore	27.08.63	03.10.63	Canada, Newfoundland
Beechmore	09.10.63	14.11.63	Canada, Newfoundland
Beechmore	21.11.63	29.12.63	Canada, Newfoundland
Carinthia	13,.01.64	26.01.64	USA

DNS: Did Not Sail